The Perfect Blend

Over 100 seriously fun vocal warm-ups

Timothy Seelig

Layout/Design: Glenn Hadsall & Joseph Rattan
Joseph Rattan Design
Photography: Shawn Northcutt Photography

Copyright © 2005, Shawnee Press, Inc.
A Division of Music Sales, Inc.
International Copyright Secured All Rights Reserved
ISBN   1-59235-094-1

TABLE OF CONTENTS

THE CHOIR

APPENDIX

ACKNOWLEDGMENTS

I Want To Thank the Academy

When I was first asked to compile a book of choral/vocal warm-ups based on my experience, my initial reaction was what most of yours would have been, "I don't know that many warm-ups. I have used the same three for years and they have done just fine." Yet, after 30 years of teaching voice, vocal pedagogy, conducting choruses and doing clinics, I came to the realization that I had better have enough in my arsenal to share with others doing the same thing I do. Just as you have done, I have picked up an array of invaluable hints and pointers all along the way.

Some of the greatest conductors on the planet have been my teachers, even though most of them, or me, for that matter, don't actually know it. But it does not lessen the impact they have had on my life. There are some great ones with whom I have studied, others I have learned from via books or videos (now even DVDs!). Others I have observed in rehearsals and performances throughout the years. Every time you hear a chorus perform, you are subconsciously cataloging things that will affect your own conducting. That is why it is difficult for us to enjoy other choral concerts. We are constantly analyzing the components of the event instead of enjoying the whole.

It boggles my mind to realize I have sung in or conducted some manner of choral group since I was, oh, three years old ("Jesus Wants Me for a Sunbeam" was my top tune). That gives me 50 years of experience. My earliest memories were of my mother, Virginia, teaching voice in the living room of our home. I was expected to occupy myself quietly as she ran her students through the drills. Apparently I was a critic at a very early age. The habit had to be broken of occasionally letting out a shrill "eeewwwww" when one of her students performed less than admirably. Mom also kept me on task as I practiced the piano. From the other room she would exclaim, "I don't hear you counting," to which I apparently replied, "I'm counting in my heart." Well, I'm still counting in my heart.

Before we get started, let me thank all of you who have contributed to this - from my earliest music teachers (Mrs. Howington in the 4th grade) to the mentors I have admired and adopted in recent years. If you see some of your exercises in this book, I hope just seeing them is flattery enough, because I sure don't remember who gave me what, much less when!

Two men have made enormous contributions to my life as a conductor. The most sensitive choral conductor I have ever known is Gerald Ray, with whom I worked at First Baptist

Church, Houston. I owe him for many incredible lessons: how a choir can deliver a text as expressively as a soloist; genius in programming; invaluable tips on memorization. And my friend Dennis Coleman of the Seattle Men's Chorus with whom I have shared most of the opinions put forth in the dogmatic chapter on "Things they don't teach you." None of us ever learned to shorten our programs, though.

In my own training as an opera singer, I have had outstanding, thoughtful vocal instruction, for which I am eternally grateful, especially Frau Professor Hanna Ludwig and Herr Professor Rudolf Knoll in Salzburg. This study has molded my teaching and conducting habits to encourage each singer to sing to the best of his or her ability. Only after that is done is it then my job to mold them into a thing called a choir.

I feel so fortunate to have had the brilliant and caring Dr. John Large and Dr. Stephen Farish as my primary professors in Vocal Pedagogy. In my 30 years of teaching that discipline, I have drawn material from countless texts. There have been a few, however, that have become a mainstay when I return to my bookshelf. A few books that are invaluable to me are:

Singing, the Mechanism and the Technic
   William Vennard

The Structure of Singing and *On the Art of Singing*
   Richard Miller

The Diagnosis and Correction of Vocal Faults
   James McKinney

Basics of Vocal Pedagogy
   Clifton Ware

Conducting Choral Music
   Robert L. Garretson

Directing the Choral Music Program
   Kenneth H. Phillips

International Phonetic Alphabet
   Joan Wall

A Musician's Soul
   James Jordan

My assumption is that you have at least one text like those above somewhere on your shelf (or attic). Dust it off. Read it. Then read this book. You cannot know too much about the vocal instrument or the way it works. This applies to how your own voice works and that of your singers. It is fundamental to the success of your chorus.

With my Vocal Ped guinea pigs: Kathryn Terrell, Michael Hamilton, Matt Lobaugh and Callie Wahl.

I must thank the incredible men and women of the Turtle Creek Chorale and The Women's Chorus of Dallas who I have conducted a total of 30 years or so. They have been patient as I searched for my own choral technique and experimented with the techniques of many others enroute. They have also taught my heart to sing along with my voice. And to my students at Southern Methodist University, some of whom are pictured in this book, thank you for keeping me on my toes. Also, my friends at the incredible Michigan State University for allowing me to try some of this out on them.

Thanks to those who read the book along the way and had the courage to say, "I have no idea what you are talking about" more than once: Reed, Lupe, Melinda, Whitney, Brad, Sam, Brandon, Kenn, Mark and Craig.

Tired of tragic old warm-ups?
Can't remember why you do them?
Are your rehearsals listless?
Do your singers fall asleep on you?
Are you pooped out?

THIS BOOK'S FOR YOU!!!
And so tasty, too.

Introduction:
let's start at at the very beginning

INTRODUCTION

Let's Start at the Very Beginning.

As I began to write, it just seemed that the correlation between music and food kept coming up. I tried to get away from it by putting down the Cheetos while I was typing (really stains the keyboard anyway). But it was impossible. Then I thought of all the choral conductors I know and realized that next to conducting, eating is what most of us love best. When music is not soothing our souls, we turn to Häagen-Dazs for comfort. So, I left the references in.

Hopefully, this book will grab your attention and not let go (and make you chuckle a bit). I hope you will keep reading just to see what fun and zany things are possible in conducting your chorus. I decided at age 35 that life was just too short not to have fun in every single thing I do: including warming up.

The book will lead you, step by step, through the basic mechanics of the voice. Once we have taken it apart, hopefully it will end up back together in one piece, more beautiful and expressive than when we started down this road together. At that point, we are going to take all of these incredible voices we have built and combine them into something called a choir!

You will be armed with more knowledge and more spice for the choral stew you are cooking up.

What This Book Is and What It Is Not.

- ✣ It is a book full of warm-ups, old and new.
- ✣ It is a book on vocal and **choral tone**.
- ✣ It is a book on vocal and **choral technique**.
- ✣ It is a book with a fresh, physical approach to singing.
- ✣ It is not a book on voice science. No muscles or ligaments.
- ✣ It is not a book on sight-reading, intonation or articulation.
- ✣ It is not a book on how to do better in contests.
- ✣ It is, above all, a good read.

Who Should Read This Book?

Well, my Mom would say everyone should, of course. I think you can look quickly at my experience and decide whether what I have to offer might fit your needs. My training in school was as a solo singer with conducting as my first related field throughout. I began teaching at the college level in 1973 and have conducted multiple choral groups every year since then. For the last 18 years, most of my work experience has been conducting volunteer/community choruses. This is completely different from a university or school setting. More on that later. Much of what is in this book is geared toward motivating the singer to greater understanding of his/her voice as it relates in a choral setting. Certainly the warm-ups work equally well for any type or age of singer.

The Answer:

✣ Anyone who sings.

✣ Anyone who conducts.

✣ Anyone whose warm-ups need a B-12 shot.

✣ Anyone who is interested in new ways to approach vocal study.

✣ Anyone looking for rehearsal tips.

✣ Anyone who is open to new programming ideas.

✣ My Mom.

Organization of the Book Is in Two Parts:

Part #1: The Voice
Part #2: The Choir

THE VOICE

Starting with the Motor, moving to the Vibrator and finally the Resonators (and Articulators) is certainly nothing new in the way of approaching the training of singers for solo or choral work. Many vocal pedagogues have used this same path. If it worked for them, it will certainly work for us. Thus, the first part of the book is divided into the following sections:

Posture (Instrument)
Motor (Breathing)
Vibrator (Vocal folds)
Resonators (Adjusting)

Other Musical Instruments

One of the most helpful discussions about the way the voice works stems from the playing of other musical instruments. Everyone in your chorus has probably played another musical instrument (other than the radio). Every single musical instrument has Motor, Vibrator and Resonator. Ask them to identify the three parts in whatever instrument they played or with which they are familiar. This little exercise will help when we transfer these concepts to their voices.

Examples:

Piano: Motor: muscle, hands
            Vibrator: strings
            Resonator: body of the piano
            and THE WORLD

Guitar: Motor: muscle/hands/fingers
            Vibrator: strings
            Resonator: body of the guitar and
            THE WORLD (all string
            instruments)

Trumpet: Motor: breath
            Vibrator: lips
            Resonator: horn and THE WORLD
            (all brass instruments)

Voice: Motor: breath
            Vibrator: vocal folds
            Resonator: throat, mouth, nose,
            THE WORLD

"Never try to teach a pig to sing. It wastes your time and annoys the pig."

Attributed to Mark Twain

THE CHOIR

Like No Other Sound on Earth

Some years ago, my chorus had a pretty high-falutin' public relations firm do a thorough "branding" of our chorus. They asked all kinds of people what their impression was of the Turtle Creek Chorale. The aim was to see what people thought of the group in order to refine our demographics and possible market segment. They came back with this: the main thing people commented on was the sound of the group. They commented on the variety of music, the significant outreach the group does throughout the community and the entertainment value attached to choral music presentations. But when asked to choose just one, it was the sound. I loved the tag line they created because it did several things. It set the standard pretty high. And it also allowed the option that if someone absolutely hated the sound, the tag line still worked. (It did not put anyone else down.) All of us have judged contests where we just didn't know what in the world to say if it was so bad. "That was like no other sound on earth" works there as well. Or "that was just breathtaking."

So, why am I telling you this? Because the sound of my choral groups drives everything I do with them, from warm-ups, to selection of repertoire to rehearsals to performances.

There is seldom a single moment when I am not thinking about how to improve the sound of the group, beginning with each singer as the building block. That is what this book is about.

> *Perfection in all musical aspects of a performance is for naught if the chorus sounds bad.*

Choral Technique

What is choral technique? Do I have one? Where can you get one? Well, the answer is, you do have one (whether you know it or not)! When asked, you might say, "I don't have a "choral technique" per se." Oh, yes you do. Whatever routine you do with your chorus on a regular basis is your choral technique, whether or not you have ever thought of it in those terms.

> *Technique is the ability to consistently repeat the same patterns of coordination.*

Whatever it is you are doing day after day, week after week, is YOUR TECHNIQUE! For better or for worse, in sickness and in health.

Given this, then, some reasonable questions are:

✢ How do you teach posture?
✢ What is the basis of your breathing technique?
✢ What do you regularly teach about registers?
✢ What is your technique regarding resonance adjustment?
✢ Have you ever just told your chorus to blend?

By the end of the book, those answers should roll off your tongue.

Teach Concepts, not Clones

One of the important warnings for us as choral conductors and vocal instructors is that we are not in the business of making the singers in our choruses sound like us. When we demonstrate, the vocal concept is what we must convey, not the actual sound they are hearing. It is important that we model technique as demonstrated in the sound and ask them to internalize and incorporate the concept, not mimic our sound. You are not the only one who needs to understand the concept behind the example. If you are able to teach your chorus the principle behind the example or the warm-up, your job will be much easier in the long run. Once you have explained the reason for doing a warm-up to your singers, it will stick with them much better than simply repeating it over and over with no reason having been given.

McPedagogy

Richard Miller calls the quick fix McPedagogy. While this is fun for your chorus and especially gratifying to the visiting clinician, it is not what will work for you in the long run. Your chorus knows when you have been to a workshop. You bring all of these great new exercises home. And you use them, for about two or three weeks. But until you internalize them by repeating them over and over, they do not actually become a part of your own "choral technique." Without understanding the long-term benefits, they will be as useful and long-lasting as hot pants and go-go boots or pet rocks.

If you don't own it,
they'll never buy it

Pendulum Theory of Production

Life is a study in balance. Vocal/Choral technique is a study in balance. Everything we attempt to teach falls along the swing of a pendulum. The pendulum at rest represents a coordinated choral technique that you have chosen as ideal for your chorus. But if your chorus is singing on one side of the pendulum, you will have to bring them all the way to the other side in order to ultimately rest in the middle. It seldom works for you to simply bring them to that middle point and expect the pendulum to stay there. If you do that, the sound will rest somewhere between where you hoped it would be and where it began. For example, your chorus is singing too white or bright a sound. You have to take them past the center, or ultimate resting point, to a darker sound than you would like in order to find that balance. Our lives are balancing acts of a pendulum in every respect. Imagine these extremes in your singers and your chorus:

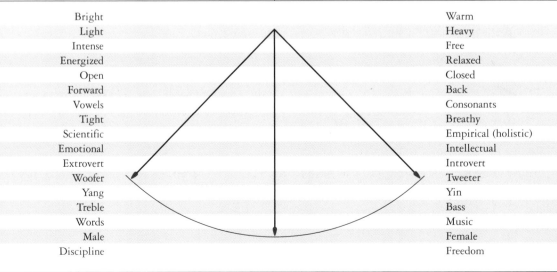

Bright	Warm
Light	Heavy
Intense	Free
Energized	Relaxed
Open	Closed
Forward	Back
Vowels	Consonants
Tight	Breathy
Scientific	Empirical (holistic)
Emotional	Intellectual
Extrovert	Introvert
Woofer	Tweeter
Yang	Yin
Treble	Bass
Words	Music
Male	Female
Discipline	Freedom

About the Exercises Themselves

It's All in a Name

Why do the exercises have such silly names? Thanks for asking. I have found that it helps in remembering them (for me and for the singers). It is so much easier to remember "Tractor Pull" than to remember "That exercise where two people pair up and face each other and try to pull each other off balance to demonstrate legato and energy in the vocal line." That is a really long name to remember.

Musical Exercises

The book may seem to have fewer musical examples than other books. Well, there is a reason for this. I know we all get in a rut regarding the actual musical sequences we use in our warm-ups, but there are only so many possibilities. Most of the exercises in this book are designed to teach technique, not ear training, not consonant building or rhythm. Those books have all been written. Therefore, most of the concepts in this book will work using the musical patterns with which you are most comfortable and that you have used throughout your career. If there is an exercise that is specifically dependent on a musical pattern, it is included. Other than that, there are just so many times you can write out a 5-note descending scale before you want to put some sharp instrument in your eye.

Vowels Referenced Are in IPA

International Phonetic Alphabet [IPA] is one of the greatest tools for any conductor or teacher. I believe that most of the references to specific vowels will be clear, even to someone who does not have a working knowledge of IPA. If not, maybe it will encourage you to get a book on IPA and learn it.

You've Got to Move

You will notice that many of the exercises in this book have accompanying hand or body movements. My choruses are accustomed to moving and using their hands or bodies. It makes the singing experience a little less esoteric and a great deal more visceral. Let them move!!! In addition (in performance), when I use a hand gesture that we have used in rehearsal, they know exactly what I am wanting... no guesswork.

We're gonna move. We're gonna touch each other. We're gonna bowl. We're gonna turn in two's and interact. You really won't achieve "oneness" or true teamwork within your chorus unless they interact with each other, not just with you! We're stepping way out of the box.

Warm 'er up (or down): there is a difference

WARM 'ER UP (OR DOWN)

There Is a Difference

Preparing your chorus to sing is one of the most important things a choral director can do. The difficulty lies in the fact that you have 20 or 200 people in front of you, each of whom is in a different state of readiness to sing and each of whom has a different level of experience. Your task is to find a median from which all of them can benefit. This is an enormous challenge.

When I conduct workshops with choruses other than mine, I tell the singers in each choir that they should never do a warm-up for which they do not know the purpose. I give them permission to kindly raise their hands and ask the conductor what a particular exercise is supposed to teach them. This sometimes causes great consternation in those conductors whose only answer is "because my high school choir teacher used it." It also causes those to sweat who either never thought of the "why" or are just using the exercises as "filler" or to kill time. "Killing time" is not an answer I would suggest you use, regardless of how true it might be.

Never do a vocalise, or ask anyone else to do one, unless you know the WHY.

Exercise 1: Taking Stock

Go through all of your books and papers and notes from college. Gather together all of the warm-ups you can. Put them all in one place. Look at them. Sort them out. Categorize them. Most importantly, figure out what each one of them achieves in the building of vocal or choral technique.

Exercise 2: Cleaning Closets!

As much as you hate cleaning your own closets, it has to be done from time to time. Think about the clothes in your closet as the warm-ups in your choral closet. You may not even remember where you got some of those things. Half of them don't fit anymore and some of them you can't imagine ever having owned in the first place. You have acquired new things along the way and pushed the old to the back thinking someday you might need them. It's time to clean the closet. If you don't know where you got a warm-up and don't know what it is for, get rid of it. If you have warm-ups in the very back of the closet that you simply do not use anymore, get them out, look at them and if they are really not useful, get rid of them. The difference here is that with clothes, if you can't use them, you should donate them to someone who can. With warm-ups, it is not a good idea. Let them go out into the universe (and not fill someone else's choral closet with junk).

Why take valuable rehearsal time with silly warm-ups anyway?

I had a young choir director in my choral techniques class say he didn't believe in warming up a choir. I about fell off my teacher's throne. What was he thinking? Well, what he was thinking is what many of you think. "I have never been given a particularly compelling reason to do warm-ups. When I have, I haven't noticed an appreciable difference and we just have too much music to learn to spend time going la la la."

The first thing I would say to anyone who thinks this, is that you cannot drag 20 or 200 people in off the street from various walks of life and just tell them to SING! It is simply not possible. Some of the reasons for doing a brief warm-up are very simple. You are the only voice teacher many or most of them have ever had! Certainly you mix vocal technique into your normal rehearsal, but they need to have some sort of grasp on how to get their instrument ready.

They bring the various ingredients — you have the recipe!

You want your singers to:

❖ Leave their worries and troubles at the door (they may decide not to pick them back up at the door when they leave).

❖ Get their blood flowing and bodies ready to sing.

❖ Breathe.

❖ Concentrate on their instrument for a moment, not notes and rhythms and text.

❖ Hear the sounds you are wanting apart from music. They can hear each other during this time, face each other or sing in two choirs.

❖ Work toward unification of vowels and concentration on intonation.

❖ Connect with each other and with you.

Just as this book does, warm-ups begin with the individuals' needs (massage, etc) and move toward preparation to be one of many in the chorus.

There is a major difference in whether you are warming up or warming down your chorus. For those of you who have 7:00 a.m. rehearsals you have one task: warming up. And bless you in it. You are taking singers from scratch (probably straight from bed) and bringing them, gently, to singing readiness. For those of you who have 7:00 p.m. rehearsals, you have one task: warming down. And bless you in it. You are taking singers from a full day of work or school and bringing their weary voices and bodies into singing readiness.

WARM-UP

Those of you who regularly deal with early morning warm-ups must have my respect and deepest sympathy. I know early church services were certainly not the brainchild of a minister of music, and rehearsals before school starts are necessary in order to get in enough rehearsal time. But, oh my, it is not easy. Two analogies will help shed some light on how important warming up in the morning really is.

You know what it's like if you put silly putty or taffy in the refrigerator. Imagine that your vocal folds are like that cold silly putty (first thing in the morning). You can't take your folds out and massage them between your warm hands, but you need to massage them to get them ready for the hurdles you are about to ask them to do.

Another analogy is to imagine you are going to run a marathon (no matter how far-fetched that may be). More important than running well is looking snappy, so you decide the day before to get new tennis shoes. On the morning of the marathon, you then decide you would really look best without socks. You start. In about 1/4 mile, you have what? Blisters. Run another quarter mile and we won't discuss what you will have done to your pretty new tennis shoes or your feet.

This is not unlike getting out of bed and singing forte first thing. The vocal folds are thick from sleep and most likely from mucous drainage. They have not functioned to phonate (speak or sing) in 8 to 12 hours. You can't begin by running a vocal marathon without eventually causing damage: blisters and more.

This is where certain techniques can aid you tremendously. I am going to tease you just a bit and leave the actual warm-ups for later chapters. But the point and the warning are meant to make you curious and a bit frightened!

In an article in the National Association of Teachers of Singing's *Journal of Singing*, world-renowned voice scientist, Dr. Ingo Titze lists his five favorite vocal warm-ups. In it, his very first suggestion is the lip trill. He lists his reasons for using this warm-up: engaging respiratory muscles quickly; minimizing force on vocal folds; spreading the vocal folds so that only the edges are vibrating; lowering the phonation threshold.

These four results of the lip trill exercise are the keys to the early morning warm-up. The bumble bee (lip trill) is the pair of thick socks to keep the tennis shoes from rubbing blisters. More on the great attributes of the lip trill later and blowing your finger.

WARM DOWN

If you are having an evening rehearsal and your singers have been talking at work all day, then your task is to warm them down, not up. They have not just crawled out of bed, but have been using their voices all day long.

Our speech therapist colleagues consistently tell us that our normal speech patterns in everyday situations cause fairly significant difficulty in speech and certainly affect our singing. Some of the things that are most egregious are:

÷ *Breathing.* We do not breathe properly when we speak, taking in just enough air to squeak by, using as little as 1/8 of our vital capacity.

÷ *Pitch.* We speak far too low. Society says women who speak low are more authoritative and smart and men who speak low are more manly.

÷ *Articulation.* We are lazy with the articulators, allowing tension to creep into our speech patterns.

That is how our singers come to us after 8 or 12 hours of work. Their vocal folds are warmed up (at least in the lower range) and don't need as much of your attention as they would in the morning hours.

The goal of warming down is focus and getting rid of a whole bunch of stuff from our lives that only become distractions to singing.

It is bringing 20 or 200 individuals into the same arena—mentally, physically, and vocally.

Just imagine for a moment the range of people you have in your chorus and how they come to you for rehearsal. You have a person who teaches school and has overexerted his/her voice for at least 8 hours. You have another who worked all day talking on the telephone. Then you have some people who do not talk all day and rarely use their voices. You have people who have stood up all day and would love a chance to sit down for awhile. You have people who have been sitting at a desk all day and would love a chance to stand. You have people who need to move around and some who need to sit still and just be quiet. You have those who live for rehearsal (we need more of those) and you have those who put up with it (and you) so they can perform. You have people for whom the music is enough and others who need the socialization. You have some who are exhausted and can barely stay awake and others who are bouncing off the walls.

And voilá, there is your chorus! And you are to be all things to all people, of course. This is where your "warming down" becomes a challenge. It is all about you, being confident in your method and engaging in your presentation. It is about your believing in yourself and in what you are going to teach them. It is about the gift you are about to give them: two hours of wonderful singing and learning and sharing.

Having considered all of the above, it is time to plan the first moments of your rehearsal.

"But I just let the chorus warm up while it is singing the repertoire. We don't have time to devote to warm-ups." You can never teach your chorus members (or a solo singer) to develop their craft to its fullest by just singing repertoire. We bring too many other distractions and issues to the actual singing of repertoire. Regardless of what language, we bring idiosyncrasies of that language to the singing. We bring emotional attachment to the test. We get distracted.

Warm-up is the only time when your singers can focus on their instrument and vocal technique without the diversions of notes, rhythms, and dynamics. Consistently beginning rehearsals with sight-singing or difficult repertoire is vocal suicide (or murder, since was your idea).

You can be a moderate success warming up your chorus on repertoire. I, personally, am a huge proponent of using repertoire to create warm-ups, as you will see. However, it requires a great deal of work and planning on your part.

In keeping with the food theme we have adopted, look at your warm-up period as if looking at a menu at an incredible restaurant where you are going to have a five-course meal. You wouldn't select five appetizers and nothing else. You want to savor each course and not skip a single one. And you don't go backwards, either. Even though you might like to start with dessert, the words of your mother come back to you, "You'll ruin your dinner!" And she was right. As you will see in the book, just as in a wonderful dinner, the order of the exercises is very important. If you choose them well and in the proper order, you will have a completely satisfying experience, at dinner or rehearsal.

When we are finished, we hope you will choose one exercise (at least) from each group, representing these areas of concern for your warm-ups:

1. **Posture (Chapter 3)**
2. **Motor (Chapter 4)**
3. **Vibrator (Chapters 5 and 6)**
4. **Resonators (Chapter 7)**
5. **Singing (Chapters 8)**

Now, grab the menu and let's talk about each course.

Posture:
holding your musical instrument

POSTURE

Holding Your Musical Instrument

You must always reserve a little time at the beginning of rehearsal before ever engaging the breathing mechanism, the vocal folds, the resonance or repertoire. Just spend some time getting focused on the body and the mind. Your singers need to relax all body parts that have become tense during the work/school day. This may take some time (and in some cases, therapy) in our high-stress world. There is a fine line between complete relaxation and rigidity. If you do not allow your singers to move, they will become rigid in almost no time. Trust me, you don't have enough time or patience to get them back from rigidity. Let their bodies move and be fluid. Let them dance.

A choir member says, "But I just want to sing!" There is so much to do before they can do that. A golfer, a tennis player or baseball player spends countless hours working on the mechanics of the swing without using a ball. The magic is in the form, the stance, the posture. There is a real correlation in singing. Entire books have been written and entire courses of study offered in just getting the body ready for singing or speaking correctly.

Many of you, like I, have had ill-fated attempts at visiting the gym to try to get in shape. Regardless of your success at this, the most often prescribed approach is to begin with the large muscle groups first and move to the smaller ones as you progress. The same is true of getting your instrument set for singing. If you do this backwards, i.e., beginning with the vocal muscle and working outward, you will be sorry when the singers begin to fatigue because their bodies were not focused, relaxed and prepared. By the time their bodies are engaged, the vocal folds are exhausted.

We like to say that the singer's musical instrument is the entire body. Unlike other instrumentalists, they do not get to put it in a case when a rehearsal or performance is over. They can't take it apart or clean it or tune it with a twist of this or that. And they can't upgrade with low-interest financing. Of all of the precious musical instruments in the world, each of your singers owns one of the most precious. Question: If you owned a priceless, irreplaceable violin, would you leave a rehearsal late on a cold night, roll down the car windows, hold the violin out the window as you drove to a smoky location to have a bite to eat and pour an alcoholic beverage over your violin and leave it out of its case the rest of the night?

Hmmmm?

Having Said That, Let's Start.

1. Faux Bubble Bath

What is the height of relaxation and decadence for most people? A nice long bubble bath with candles, soft music, etc.

Exercise: Ask your singers to close their eyes and imagine this (or a similar) experience and simply sit quietly for a moment. Ask singers to notice normal breathing patterns. With each easy breath, they become more relaxed and their breathing deepens.

2. Clear Out the Cobwebs

While the singers are relaxing, give them a "focus" word that will be important in the evening's rehearsal. That can be anything from peace, relax, enjoy, round sound, sharing, etc. With each breath, the focus word is repeated mentally. The goal: shut out the world for the next few hours.

3. Cheap Massage

This is one of the exercises that everyone does, but may not think about the many good things that result. Sure, it relaxes the shoulders and the body. Sure, it helps get the body involved and energized. But it also breaks down all kinds of invisible barriers between people in your chorus. The neck is great, the hairline is great (unless you have too many members with hairpieces, wigs or toupees). You know the drill: have them turn in lines and do a little massaging. Ask them all to lean back into the person massaging them. Music accompanying this can be fun. "About face. Repeat exercise."

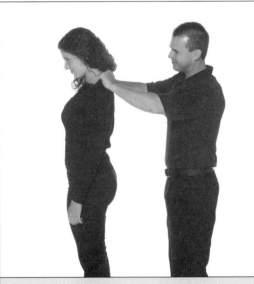

Cheap Massage

4. Karate Kid

Add a soft karate chop across the shoulders and back to your massage. This is a fun time to have the singers sing an "[a]…" it will be a very relaxed sound WITH VIBRATO! They can yawn and sigh and make all kinds of noises while being chopped. It is somewhat like singing into a fan when you were a kid.

Karate Kid

5. Pat-Down

This is a really fun addition to the above exercise. After the massage and the karate, have the singers "pat themselves down" as done in the airport or during an arrest.

Starting with both hands patting, you can move up and down the front of your body from belly to thighs to ankles and then up the back from ankles to bottom and then up to the shoulders, the cheeks and the top of the head. I watched Sean Vogt do this with the Michigan State University Glee Club and they had a blast.

6. Loosen Up

You can start at the floor and work up or vice versa. Step lightly. Shake your feet. High step. Bend at the waist. Reach to the sky. Reach to the floor and shake your hands. Roll your shoulders up and around, front to back and drop them back. Do the opposite just to show your singers how horrible they look and feel when they drop their shoulders forward. Roll your head around gently. Squeeze your face together. Look surprised. Then stick your tongue out and in quickly. When you don't feel very creative, pull out some childhood songs: "The Hokey Pokey," "I'm a Little Teapot," "The Itsy Bitsy Spider." You'll be surprised how much fun it can be and they'll think you are a genius.

What if the Hokey Pokey IS what it's all about?

7. Give Yourself a Hug

It is great to end the massage, karate, and hokey with a really great hug of yourself. This is just another exercise that stretches and relaxes the back and shoulder muscles while making people smile. If you have a group that can handle some fun, tell them to go ahead and hug the person next to them.

Big Hugs

*Giving and getting
enough hugs
IS what it's all about!*

8. "Stand up straight"

How many times did your Mom say that to you? And so you attach some fairly negative internal responses to those instructions. It is our job to convey that message, without using those words! Imagine you are a puppet with the string attached to the back of the head, lifting the entire body, elongating the spine. Reach for the sky, drop the arms. Stand tall while lowering the chin slightly. Our challenge is to find more interesting ways to achieve good posture. One of those is the use of mirrors.

Stand Up

One person's chest heaving with inhalations while singing is unsightly. Get 20 or 50 or 200 in matching outfits and let them all heave and it becomes either hilarious or a good way to make the audience seasick.

9. Body Alignment

Give your singers the following directions.

Feet…8 inches apart, one slightly in front
    of the other
Knees…slightly bent
Thighs…push down on them in your mind
Pelvis…tucked in slightly
Chest…high and expanded
Chin…just below horizontal
Head…erect
Mind…engaged
Face…smiling

When you are finished, they should feel completely out of whack. Then ask them to shake all of that out and try to get back to that very out of whack position, but in a more relaxed sense.

10. Share in Love

Have the chorus number 1–2, 1–2 across the room. Ask the "ones" to face the "twos" and have them critique each other's posture. We'll do this again several times with several different purposes, so they need to get used to the numbering system. This can begin with each one checking the posture of their "partner" and making constructive suggestions about how they might improve.

head up   head down   head up
[a]

Music Exercise 1: Nine-note scale, sung on [a]

11. Kindergarten fix

Blame it on kindergarten. One of my most important realizations is that everything I learned wrong about vocal technique, I learned from my kindergarten teacher. That, of course, is not true; many other teachers helped. Assigning blame is so comforting. But something really frightening stuck in my brain when she stood in front of the class and used her hand to denote the movement of the pitches on "Row, row, row your boat." She started with her hand low for the low notes, much like Shirley Temple in an early movie, and with each pitch higher, her hand moved

up until we were all singing the top "merrily" with our chins raised happily toward the heavens! This is a subconscious habit not easily broken. But we must try.

🏃 *Exercise:* Sing an ascending/descending nine-note scale. At the beginning, the head should be allowed to gently rest completely back (looking at the ceiling). As you ascend, the head moves downward so that by the time you get to the top of the octave, the chin is almost resting on the sternum. Then reverse the action. After you have done this a couple of times, have your chorus

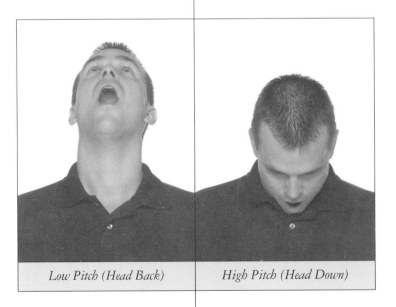

Low Pitch (Head Back)   *High Pitch (Head Down)*

do it the other way. You need not say a thing, they will immediately know how many ways of wrong that is. The head dropped gently back for the low notes releases tension in the larynx. The head resting on the sternum for the high notes avoids the tension created by a high larynx and chin.

Legend has it that the true Russian basses developed their extended lower ranges by the technique of resting the head back as they descended into lower ranges during training.

12. Kindergarten Applied

Find a leap in a piece of music. If it is an ascending leap, ask the chorus to move their heads (chins) downward for the upper note. If it is descending, reverse the action. They will soon understand the pattern of not raising their heads (chins) for high notes or lowering them for the low notes.

13. Sternum Power

I love to give power to body parts that you ordinarily might not think of as powerful. Most often we connect raising the chest with inhalation. We also connect exhalation with a dropping or sagging chest. This exercise will help separate those thoughts.

1. One hand on sternum.
2. Exhale, collapse and bend over.
3. Without inhaling, stand erect, regal.
4. Inhale. Sternum power
5. Exhale while pushing your hand up with your chest.

| *Hand on Sternum* | *Bend Over, Exhale* | *Stand Tall, Then Inhale* |

This is when you really empower your sternum. As you exhale and push up, the rib cage will rise, pushing the hand up. There is really no way for it to work the other way around, with the hand pushing or pulling the sternum upward.

14. Raggedy Ann/Andy

This is simply an exercise that you can cater to your own group and your own style. The whole point is relaxation of the entire body. Ask your singers to go completely limp, like a rag doll. Depending on the age and flexibility of your chorus members, this can go as far as bending completely over to touch the floor (only a memory for most of us). Shake the hands. Roll back up gently into a relaxed stance. As your singers get back into a singing position, the last thing to fall into alignment is the head, finishing off the stretching of the spine.

Tired

Perky

Exercise 15: Dive Up

Exhale while clasping and raising your hands above the head. Inhale. Feel the low expansion of the abdomen with the breath. Exhale on a hiss as you drop hands to sides. Pay close attention that the chest remains as high as possible. You will feel the dramatic inward movement of not just the abdomen, but the back as well.

16. Elbow Windmill

Place your hands behind your head, elbows out. Exhale as you do this. Then, inhale deeply. First, do the windmill turning from side to side. Then, as you exhale, pull in the arms to where the elbows are touching in front of your face. Hold the exhalation. Then, on cue, spread the elbows out with a huge inhalation.

Dive Up

Elbow Windmill

17. Standing Sit-up

None of us really wants to do real sit-ups, so here is a simulation that won't hurt us by getting our abs in shape! Raise your elbows much like they were in the previous exercise, but with the hands behind the head and the elbows forward. Take a deep breath. As you simulate the sit-up by bending over, exhale. Come back up. Inhale deeply. Repeat once or twice. It is a great exercise to feel the expulsion of the air, then the ability to stand erect without inhaling. The breaths should be very deep and well-coordinated.

Stand as if you were taller, sing as if you were fatter!

Standing Sit-Up

CHAPTER 3

Motor:
rev your
engines

MOTOR: REV YOUR ENGINES

"There is no such thing as breath support. It is all breath pacing."

Clifton Ware

We do not comprehend how incredibly physical is the steady, healthy isometric muscle tension of the entire instrument. It is required to provide a complete support system, not just a muscle here or there, to ensure vocal freedom.

So, you are driving along on the freeway and your car stops and you are going to be late for rehearsal and you haven't really planned it all that well because you were going to get there 10 minutes early and that was going to be plenty of time to plan your two-hour rehearsal and grab a Diet Coke and a Snickers bar. You are completely frustrated. You get out of your car and by the time you figure out how to open the hood and look inside, you are reminded that you don't really know what all that stuff is anyway, so that was fairly futile. You call for help. Help arrives. After checking spark plugs, battery, dip stick, carburetor, etc. the diagnosis arrives: you are simply out of gas… didn't check that.

The same illogical process is true with malfunctions in the voice. This is exactly what we do as voice technicians. A singer comes to us, or all of our singers come to us, with vocal issues. We begin to tinker under the hood without checking the motor. We begin with the "mask" resonance. We move from that to the tongue tension and to all manner of other misguided methods we learned from our teachers, who learned it from their teachers, who learned it… And we forget to check the gas gauge: the breath! If your singers are having any vocal issues, go there first!

Babies Breathe Perfectly.

So what happened? Well, it seems to me, when we stood for the first time, our first thought was probably, "Do I look fat in these diapers?" Of course, no one could look thin in a diaper. From that moment, we began holding in our stomachs, whether to look thin or because of a suck-in-your-gut military breath or corsets worn by women (and some men) at various times in history. It doesn't matter. When told to stand tall and breath in, most people on the street will pull in their abdomen. Whatever the original cause, it is all wrong. You cannot look thin and take a good breath.

Inner Tube

When the diaphragm (the partition that is the floor to the chest and the ceiling to the abdomen) descends with a full breath, the "inner-tube" that surrounds your mid-section expands. That is a simplified version of what happens, but unless you experience expansion around your middle, you aren't breathing correctly. And, we can be fairly certain the chests of your singers are heaving. The inner tube surrounds your mid-section.

Three Directions Describing the Breath and Its Results:

In, Down, and Out

It can't be any other combination. One favorite to try is:

In, Up, and In

Breathing is an interactive and very physical contest between the elevation of the chest and ribs and the support of the abdominal muscles. They are both equally critical to efficient inhalation and exhalation. You can hold air in the lungs for a long time by inhaling and shutting off the glottis. This gets you absolutely nowhere in regards to building breathing muscles for singing. However, expanding the chest, breathing deeply and holding that breath without closing the vocal folds is another thing altogether. This is the proper breathing technique, the result of which will be discussed in a bit.

There are two simultaneous battles going on to make breathing truly work. The first is that of the internal intercostal muscles (and gravity) working against your efforts to keep your chest raised and expanded. The second is the battle of the abdominal muscles to keep the inner tube from collapsing too quickly, ultimately allowing you no control over the air in your lungs when the diaphragm is elevated.

There isn't much of a battle going on in our normal breathing. Quiet, at-rest breathing is what we do most of our lives; in fact, approximately 20,000 times each 24-hour period. For singing, we must change that completely. And the body is not all that happy at what you are requiring of it.

So, breathe, breathe, breathe. Let's go.

1. Sternum Power: see page 21

Return to this exercise and use it to work on breathing as opposed to posture.

2. Farinelli

This is an incredible exercise that has multiple positive benefits. It has been attributed to the famous castrato, Farinelli. It trains both the muscles of inhalation as well as exhalation. It will increase the amount of air, vital capacity, the singer takes into lungs. It teaches suspension of the breath without closing the glottis. It teaches the sensations of singing without using the vocal folds. Once mastered, it can revolutionize the way your chorus uses its breath. Those are strong statements, but this is one of the only exercises that I feel comes with a guarantee: to increase lung capacity used in singing.

Exercise: Have singers turn a quarter of a turn toward the center. Now, as you count to 8, they raise their arms to shoulder height and gently inhale THE ENTIRE 8 COUNTS. When they get to the top, at count eight, make sure they keep their glottis (vocal folds) open. Ask them to pant lightly, then roll their shoulders around in a circle front to back, then take another good "cup" or "pint" of air, pant a little more, then begin the lowering of arms and exhale. Have them exhale on one of the following; Hiss; zzzzz; a long slow hummed portamento, and finally, on a familiar song or one you are working on. While they are exhaling or singing, you instruct them to keep their chests raised and not pull in the abdomen too soon or quickly. When they have finished the exercise, they should be in a perfect position to sing. Have them take a quick, low breath and blow it out. Start again.

Warning: only do this 3 or 4 times in a row or you'll faint. According to legend, the famous castrato Farinelli did this exercise for long periods of time each day. He didn't have much else to do.

Inhale up to Eight.

Exhale on a Hiss

Arms to Sides, Chest Raised

3. Prep Breath

Take any piece of music with an introduction of two or more measures. Have your chorus breathe for eight beats prior to entry. You will be surprised at how beautiful the attack will be and how relaxed it is. Warning: Do not have them breathe too soon, and hold the breath by closing their folds until their entrance. It won't be pretty. It is difficult to start the breath flow again. The inhalation and phonating process should feel like one constant circle motion without a stop at the peak of inhalation. You can begin to train your chorus not to gasp in the last nanosecond before singing with a simple gesture of raising your hand or hands in an upward motion for however many beats you intend them to inhale.

Prep Breath

4. Italian Breath

The international Italianate school touts an exercise of blowing out 6–8 candles in succession. This is a great warm-up to precede panting exercises. Once you have done the blowing out, I would challenge you to exercise the opposite set of muscles as well, sucking in 6–8 times as well. This is more difficult than it sounds.

5. Dog Breath

Panting has always been a useful and popular activity before singing. I find it best to do this with a hand on the sternum and one on the abdomen. This way the singer can keep tabs on his/her own success. Because of the "looking thin" thing, they may be panting backwards, pulling in on inhalation. The hands help monitor this. Begin the panting very slowly, increasing the pace only as fast as they can master it. This exercise also releases some of the tension gathered during the day when we are not breathing deeply.

6. Savings Plan

All too often, when singing the chorus will simply begin a phrase not being conscious of the breath requirements soon to be demanded of them. Most often, this is the cause of running out of breath on a challenging phrase.

Exercise: Select a familiar song your chorus can sing from memory, or a phrase from a piece they are working on. First, ask them to sing the phrase while using most of their breath in the first half. This will allow them to feel the wasted breath and how the end of a phrase feels when starved for air. Then, ask them to repeat the same phrase, consciously using only 1/4 of their air in the first 1/2 of the phrase, saving 3/4 of their air for the last half of the phrase. You, and they, will be amazed at how this simple equation will help their consciousness of the breath savings plan, instead of blowing it all on the first part of the phrase.

7. Fountain of Youth

Any beautiful tone rests on the breath, floats on the breath, and is nourished by the breath. To demonstrate, put one hand lightly over your upward-pointed index finger. Your finger represents breath flow, your hand the vocal folds. There is a balance of light pressure from the breath (finger) that simply supports the hand. If there is too much pressure from the breath, the vocal folds (as shown by the hand) either respond with tension, or the hand will go flying upward. If there is too much weight in the hand, it stifles the breath flow. Picture a fountain with a ball of some sort at the top of the water flow, perched perfectly as the water supports it. Too much or too little flow ruins the effect. Same with the breath.

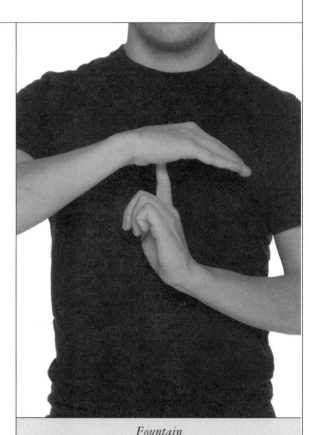

Fountain

Exercise: Ask singers to sing a chord on pitches in a comfortable range. Have them place one hand resting gently on the upturned index finger of the other hand. As they sing, ask them to mash down on the index finger as they sing and imitate that sound. Then, have them push breath through to make a breathy sound, thus pushing the hand upward and off the flow of air. This will demonstrate for them what steady air pacing should feel and sound like.

Back Expansion

8. Back Stretch

Have singers sit on the edge of their chairs, bent forward with their elbows on knees. Ask them to inhale deeply. Because they have constricted the available space in the abdominal area, they will notice significant back expansion. Do this several times. Then ask them to stay seated and place their hands on their lower back to feel the expansion. Again, repeat. Next, have them stand, lean forward slightly, hands on lower back, and do the same thing. Finally, have them stand up straight and repeat, filling the entire inner tube.

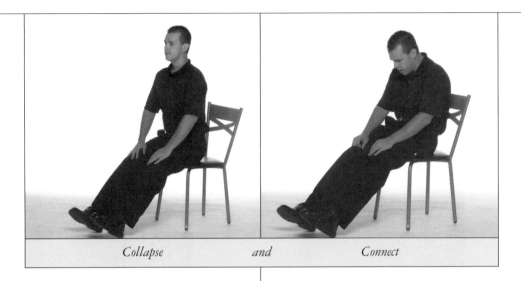

Collapse *and* *Connect*

9. Collapse and Connect

The connecting of breath and sound is crucial. Some call this "hooking up the breath." This is much like the standing sit-up, but seated. While singers are seated on the edge of the chair, have them inhale deeply, then collapse as they exhale. Ask them to sit back up, inhale, and this time, sigh as they collapse. Finally, ask them to sit up, inhale, and do a descending portamento. At this point, they should feel the connection of air to sound. Have them stand, inhale, and collapse as they sigh. Once again, with a sung portamento. Even though we are only working on breath at this moment, when you add voice to this exercise, you are showing your singers a wonderful concept called "appoggio." This is the Italian word meaning "to lean." This is the wonderful moment when the airflow meets the vocal folds, in perfect combination with only enough tension present to phonate. It is a wonderful feeling for the folds to be this free before we get in the way with our preconceived ideas of how we should sound and how we should sing.

10. The Dynamic Duo: Yawn and Sigh

You can't have one without the other. Simple as these two may be, they are indicators of many other things. No sigh? Tight sound. No yawn? Closed throat. More on that later.

Exercise: ask singers to imitate the feeling they have when stifling a yawn (like in rehearsal when they don't want you to think they are bored). Feel the exaggerated relaxation in the throat. Then, simply make up a pitch and fall off it just as they do when they are yawning.

Swimming Breath

11. Swimming Breath

This is great fun. Have your singers bend forward at the waist as if swimming under water. They are going to swim the entire length of the pool in one breath. They swim and swim and swim until they can take it no more and they must come up for air, gasping for breath, but with the lips in an [o] shape. When using this as a breathing exercise, the singers will sense the complete depletion of the breath upon exhalation (as if underwater). As they come out of the "water," they will then feel the immediate intake of air. The exercise is not only fun, but one everyone can relate to in their own life. This will be a huge and wonderful, deep breath. Thanks to Jing Ling Tam for this.

a Rose

12. A Rose Is a Rose

Someone very special has given you the most beautiful rose in the world. While its beauty astounds you, you simply must smell it. There is no way you cannot inhale deeply. Have your singers imagine this by actually pretending to hold the rose to their nose, close their eyes and inhale deeply to take in every bit of the fragrance they can. There is something about filling the nostrils and the lifting mask, and then the deep breath that cannot be duplicated any other way. It is also very relaxing and soothing at the same time.

13. A Cool Spot

Take that same feeling in Exercise 12, but now breathe through the mouth, this time remembering the depth of the breath and the path it took. The point is to adjust the mouth and throat so that the inhalation causes a cool sensation in the back of the throat—very high, right past the arched soft palate. If you want to show them another way, ask them to use a very lazy throat position and breath. No cool spot anymore.

14. Nose Breathing for Singing

Books have been filled and treatises written on the do's and don'ts of nose breathing while singing. Obvious don'ts include the fact that you can't get as much air through the nose quickly enough. It can be noisy and if you breath really quickly and deeply, you risk one of the nostrils actually sticking shut, which is not attractive at all. On the other hand, the nose breath is often more relaxed and results in a deeper breath than a quick through-the-mouth breath. It is also used to focus the singer's attention on the "smiling" mask area of the face. There is, of course, the issue of the relaxed/lowered position of the soft palate when breathing through the nose, but we'll ignore that for now. I believe a quiet nose breath at the beginning of a piece or in an interlude can relax and reset the breathing mechanism.

 Exercise: Select a piece of music with several substantial interludes. Ask your singers to nose breathe in each of them. See if you notice a difference in a more relaxed onset of tone.

15. Four Stages of Breathing

Inhalation, Suspension, Exhalation and Recovery

It is critical that your singers understand and work on the suspension portion of the breath. There are many ways to do this, but the simplest is as follows:

 Exercise: Stand tall; raise the chest; take a wonderful breath, as if through a straw, filling the entire inner tube and have them hold that breath for whatever period of time you choose, without closing the glottis. They will feel the muscles rebelling. When the singers are about to rebel, allow them to exhale.

Valve vs. Phonation

In most of the animal kingdom, what we call the vocal folds function only as a valve for two functions: to protect the lungs from particles entering them and to hold air in the lungs for activities akin to lifting heavy things, childbirth or other functions that require exertion.

You can demonstrate that for yourself by pretending to lift something heavy while closing your vocal folds (glottis). These are the biological functions of the folds. Humans have added the function of phonation for communication. The two need to be distinguished as much as possible. If one does not breathe properly, with the appropriate combination of chest expansion and abdominal muscle support, then the folds must act as a valve to keep the air in while also trying to phonate freely.

16. Valve Job

The muscular forces and elastic properties of the folds (myoelastic) make it possible for a singer to close the vocal folds and for them to stretch to pitches dictated by messages from the brain. You can open and close the glottis without any thought of pitch. We do that every single day.

Exercise: Ask your singers to take a deep breath and close the glottis (if you demonstrate, they won't be frightened by that funny word). Have them hold their breath for a bit. They will see that it takes no muscle activity at all, except for the miniscule stretching of the vocal folds. It will not help them develop breathing for singing. The vocal folds are only working as a valve.

17. Suction Action

Airflow properties (aerodynamic) make it possible for the vocal folds to come together through the Bernoulli principal (see below).

Exercise: This time, take a deep breath but do not close the glottis. The glottis (vocal folds) remains open, allowing the singers to feel the sensations of the breathing musculature holding air in the lungs, without the valve allowing complete control of breath pacing. Hold for a moment. As they exhale, have them begin with a sigh and add voice halfway through. There is no grabbing of the vocal folds, they simply join in.

The Bernoulli principal is an aerodynamic principle that states air in motion will bring the vocal folds together due to decreased air pressure of molecules in motion. The folds are gently brought together and puffs of air build up below them and begin the opening and closing process. You can read much more about it in your voice science book.

18. Chattanooga Choo Choo

Getting the breath activated along with the articulators is always a challenge. One fun way to do that is through train noises.

Exercise: Begin slowly as if the train were just leaving the station on a whispered sound "chooga, chooga, chooga, chooga." Singers may breathe when they need to as the train speeds up. End the exercise with the train whistle, which of course throws them into a wonderful head voice (light mechanism).

19. Pssst. Shhh....

A little further work on connecting the breath with consonants is one where the singers try to get the attention of those across the room to tell them to be quiet. This is a scene out of real life.

Exercise: Two big psst's and a long shhh should do the trick quite nicely.

20. Air Elevator

The air elevator can be at the ground floor, or any floor higher. Obviously we are hoping that the air elevator always starts at the ground floor, which is ostensibly at "fig leaf" level. Inhalation begins on the top floor. Place the hand horizontally in front of the mouth or nose (whichever orifice you are using to breathe). As you inhale, the elevator descends to the ground floor, with your hand showing the descent of the elevator itself. When the elevator has hit the ground floor, it is ready to rise again with the exhalation of the breath. It doesn't stay at ground level for very long. In singing a phrase, the elevator rises slowly with the use of air.

Elevator

CHAPTER 4

Vibrator:
      the most
powerful
           3/4 inch
in the world...
                 (the vocal folds)

VIBRATOR

The Most Powerful 3/4 Inch in the World

One of our main tasks as vocal coaches is to remove as much tension from the entire vocal instrument as possible. The "natural" voice is pretty spectacular. And most of us have spent years adding layer upon layer of adjustments and manipulations, trying to achieve a sound that may not be who we really are at all. Our job is to remove as much of that as possible, peeling away the layers to get back to free, relaxed production, while retaining the energy and intensity in our art form. Not an easy task.

Most of us grew up calling those little things that help us make a lot of noise, "vocal cords." That terminology is perfectly acceptable, although it does leave the impression that there are two strands of something suspended over a cavernous opening. "Vocal folds" is more descriptive of what they really look like. One of the most amazing realizations for singers is the actual size of the folds. They are only 1/2 to 3/4 of an inch long! And to think what comes from those tiny folds literally changes the world every day, for good or bad. It can hurt feelings or soothe them; can start wars or end them; can encourage your singers or devastate them.

Have you ever wondered what vocal folds sound like if not attached to a body? It is a rather pitchless buzz or, if taken to the extreme, like putting your tongue between your lips and blowing (raspberry). That is the basic sound at the point of the glottis. Humbling, huh? We have specific work to do with the vocal folds, for sure. Most of that is in finding the precise balance of relaxation and good tension through air pacing. But as teacher/conductor, we can't change the innate quality of our singers' vocal folds. We are, however, responsible for the development of the sound that eventually emerges. The ultimate sound your singers make depends on so much more than that basic vibratory sound emitting from their folds.

What does that mean to you? It means that you, the teacher/conductor, are then responsible for the development of the voices your singers entrust to you. Once you have helped them to laryngeal freedom, the real work begins: Coloring! Certainly you cannot teach each of them individually, but your instruction will ultimately result in how they sing, individually as well as in a group.

As stated earlier in the book, when you do add vocal folds to the warm-up, you need to do so with great care and attention. The onset of tone should only follow focus on the flow of air. Beginning all warm-up sessions with breath work will help attain that freedom of tone we are seeking. The breathiness in the warm-up period can always be removed later when singing repertoire. It is much easier to do that than reverse tight, hyperfunctional singing.

> ### *"The breath should feel as if it is on fast forward rather than play."*
>
> Virginia Dupuy

Any exercise you can use to get the breath flowing is important because:

1. We don't breathe correctly in our daily lives.
2. These exercises keep the folds from slamming together during warm-ups.
3. Additional airflow aids in thinning the folds for easier range extension.

And finally, we get to sing our exercises!

1. Bobbing for Apples

Most amateur singers do not have a concept of where the vocal folds actually are. They stretch from front to back just behind the Adam's apple. They also have no real concept that there are three complete systems beginning in the front, with the larynx/trachea moving back to the esophagus and finally to the spinal column.

They also do not have any clue as to how small the folds are.

Exercise: Have your singers find their Adam's apples (larynx). Some, especially women, will have to swallow or yawn to find it. Some of our older singers will have to count down to just below chin number 3. By using a yawn or back of the tongue motion, see if they can manipulate their Adam's apple up and down.

Bobbing

Pitch Changer

2. Pitch Changer

Find the Adam's apple and place the fingers on it as if pinching. Sing a medium pitch. Push in gently. The pitch will lower. Release the Adam's apple suddenly, and pitch will rise. This will show the singer where the folds are located, running front to back and how sensitive they are. Pitch determination is a front to back thing, not up and down.

3. Kill the Scoop

There are only a few people in the world who truly cannot match pitch. Explaining the process to your singers in a simple way can help them be confident in hitting a pitch dead center. The process exhibits an incredible series of events. Sound waves from the source disturb the air and reach the ear. The ear sends the message to the brain, the message is then translated into a pitch and that information is sent to the vocal folds. They stretch to exactly that pitch instantaneously. When a singer listens carefully to a pitch, the vocal folds are simply ready for that singer to apply air and sing that pitch. If there is scooping or wandering, it is most likely a product of lack of concentration on the part of the singer. This is not a muscle problem, but concentration. Once a singer understands this and trusts his/her ear, much of the problem can be avoided.

🏃 *Exercise:* Choose a pitch. Ask the singers to first scoop up to it, then slide down to it. Lastly, have them sing the pitch on dead center. It is a concentration thing. (See Music Exercise 2.)

Music Exercise 2: Matching Pitch

[a]　　　　　　[a]　　　　　　[a]

THE FOLLOWING THREE EXERCISES ARE DEFINITELY IN THE MORNING WARM-UP ROUTINE.

4. Bumble Bee

One of the most popular exercises for singers is the Bumble Bee or lip trills, although I am not sure most know exactly what the benefits are. Some of the benefits are listed earlier in the book as outlined by Dr. Ingo Titze. The ways this can be used are only limited by your own imagination. Every song, every arpeggio, every scale can be sung with the lip trill. Some singers may have difficulty actually keeping the lips buzzing. In that case, move to the next exercise suggestion. You'll see the Bumble Bee again in the section on Registers as it is a versatile little exercise. (See Music Exercise 3.)

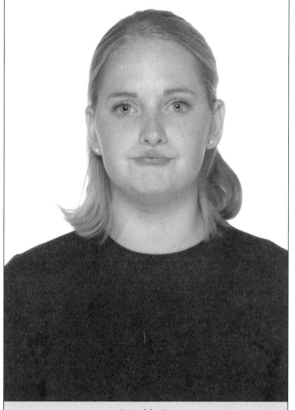

Bumble Bee

Music Exercise 3: Octave Slide

lip trill

5. Finger Blow

Another way to achieve much of the same effect as the Bumble Bee, without wearing out the lips, is to have the singers hold their finger in front of their mouths (as if blowing it out) while they vocalize or sing selections from the repertoire on the [u] vowel. The point is to actually feel (and hear) the additional breath being used. When the vocal folds tighten or the singer backs off the breath, there will be no air on the finger and no noise, thus indicating lack of breath flow. The added benefit is that once a singer is able to sing a phrase while blowing his/her finger, and then the finger is removed, there is normally no issue whatsoever in singing that phrase with ample breath and with efficient vocal tone.

Business Card

Finger Blow

6. Get Down to Business

One of the other ways to get the same result is to hold a piece of paper or business card in front of the mouth and make it buzz while singing. The real test, however, is whether or not you can whistle and sing at the same time. Only for the very advanced and adventuresome.

7. Attack of the Three Bears

One of the first things to address after your singers are breathing perfectly is the onset of tone or the addition of tone to breath. There are three kinds of attack (and also release). Goldilocks says:

"Oooo, that attack is too breathy." (hypofunctional)

"Ow-w-w, that attack is too tight." (hyperfunctional/glottal)

"Ah, that attack is just right." (coordinated, dynamic)

In the warm-up period, it is fine to do some pretty hypofunctional (breathy) singing.

Exercise: Select a chord. Have the singers sing it extremely breathy. Then have them inhale and close the glottis and sing the chord, squeezing on the breath and using as little as possible. Finally, have them sing the chord using only the slightest bit of imaginary [h] just as the vocal folds come together to make the sound. That attack is "just right."

Note: If there is a sudden release of air when your singers cut off a forte chord, they are singing in a hyperfunctional manner and this needs to be addressed.

8. The Scream

Place your hands on each side of your face. Use a descending five-note scale. Begin the tone with an elongated, one full second aspirate [h], followed by a nice relaxed [a], asking your singers to pay close attention to the actual onset of the tone when the vocal folds come together in perfect "tension" against the breath. Go up by half steps. We looked briefly at the Bernoulli principle in Chapter 4, Exercise 17. By this principle, the air in motion through the vocal folds causes the folds to come gently together as it passes, creating a perfect "attack" with an imaginary [h]. (See Music Exercise 4.)

Hands on Side of Face

Music Exercise 4: Five-Note Descending Scale. Ascending by 1/2 Steps.

Ha _____

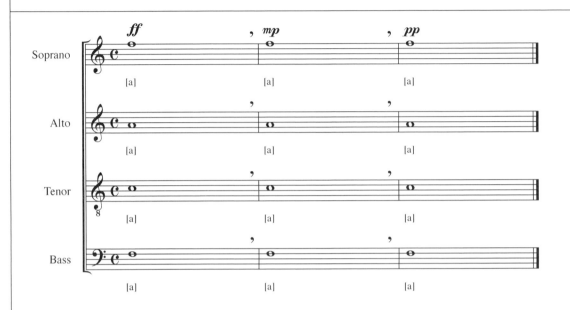

Music Exercise 5: Various Attacks

9. Bowling Ball or Feather

When you are teaching your singers how to actually begin a tone, it is useful to have them place a hand, palm up, perpendicular to the floor. In the other hand, have them imagine various items that will simply, but very graphically, demonstrate the different kinds of attack you might be looking for. For the forte or fortissimo attack, ask them to imagine a bowling ball in the right hand as it lands on the outstretched left hand. Then a softball. Then a Ping-Pong ball. Finally, a feather. Practicing the different levels of attack, you will have a fantastic variety of possibilities without having to describe it each time you want to use it. (See Music Exercise 5.)

Bowling Ball

Feather

10. A B Cs

This is a great exercise to work on the folds to just phonate, not serve as a valve. The point is to hold air in the reservoir and allow the folds the freedom they need and deserve.

Exercise: Stand tall, chest expanded and raised. Place hands on the inner tube and inhale deeply all the way around your middle. Sing the alphabet on a medium pitch with a beautiful, supported tone. Try to keep the inner tube inflated for as long as possible (coach the singers as they do this) and keep the chest lifted. The inner tube should stay expanded as you sing. When the air is almost gone (or they think it is), allow them to deflate the inner tube, but never collapse the chest. Do it again and see if you can add letters to the alphabet without scrimping on air and without sacrificing tone quality. The same exercise works with counting, singing a familiar song such as "America the Beautiful," "Happy Birthday," or a song from your repertoire.

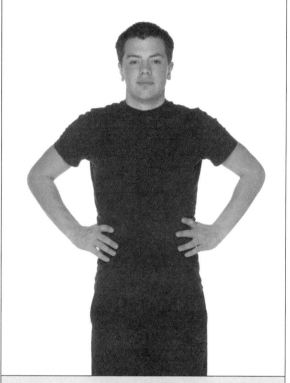

Inner Tube

11. Breath Pacing

Use the preceding exercises, but allow the singers to use three speeds of air pacing. The first will use almost no breath. They will note how much longer they can sing, and also how ugly it is. Then ask them to sing it as breathy as they possibly can. They will obviously run out of air very, very quickly. The third way (the "just right") will demonstrate for them the proper pacing of their air.

Other End of the Breath Pendulum

There have been a great number of exercises aimed at getting the breath moving. This is certainly a priority for adult singers, and especially amateurs who do not sing for a living. I believe most of our adult choruses have issues with the lack of breath flow. However, you may have individual singers who have a breathy tone quality or you may want to help your chorus in certain instances move toward a less "airy" sound. In that case, the following are suggestions.

12. Vocal Fry

Most of the previous exercises are designed to get the breath flowing at a steady pace. If your chorus or some singers cannot seem to phonate in an efficient way—in other words, sing breathy—the following is an exercise for them.

When you first roll over in the morning and the realization dawns that you have something to do that day that is not too thrilling, what is the first sound you make? It is that gravely noise that uses almost no air and has no discernable pitch. It also conveys a myriad of emotions with no words. This is a sound one should not make too often for the reasons stated earlier in the warning about new tennis shoes with no socks. The vocal folds slam together because there is not enough air present and you are in the bottom

of the range. However, this can be a tool to use when the sound is breathy and there is nothing else to do about it.

 Exercise: Have the singer do the vocal fry. Play a pitch in mid-range and ask the singer to slowly slide up to that pitch. The singer will notice exactly when the "good tension" in the vocal folds lets go to the lax, breathy sound. Knowing and feeling is the first step to repairing. It is also a fun exercise for the choir in general. Use sparingly. This exercise encourages the vocal folds to vibrate against one another in a fairly dramatic way. Not as detrimental as coughing or clearing the throat, but still not something one would want to do excessively.

13. Hummers

We have all worked on humming exercises to get the bones in the head buzzing in forced resonance with the tone. Any of these exercises are good to experience these sensations.

 Exercise: select any musical pattern or phrase from repertoire and sing it on [m], [n], or [ŋ]. One reminder: it is easy to use very little breath when humming like this. Work against this tendency. The [m] allows for a relaxed jaw. The [n] allows for a tone more focused behind the teeth (alveolar ridge). The [ŋ] will provide the most buzz for the money. (See Music Exercise 6.)

[m] _____

Music Exercise 6: Use [m], [n] or [ŋ]

14. Hum Focus

This is a great opening warm-up when adding the vocal folds. Have the entire chorus hum together on a unison pitch around, perhaps, a G. Have them feel the hum in different spaces and different dynamics. Basses and altos drop to a 5th below. Tune this. Let them enjoy this "drone." You can allow them to open to various vowels. Then return to the hum and then to unison. Then sopranos and tenors go up a 5th and the process is repeated until you come back to unison. It is great for tuning, for unification, resonances and a bunch of other purposes. Thanks, David Rayl.

Octaves Get Their Own Three Pages!

I love singing octaves (or other leaps for ear training purposes).
Almost every singer, young or old, has "high note" issues. Somehow (and it could have been those pesky kindergarten teachers), we have either a fear of high notes or a feeling we can conquer them if we put enough muscle underneath them or enough tension surrounding them!

Here are several exercises that will help your singers break down their fear of high notes, and reinforce the concept that high notes are down and low notes are up!

15. Show Me the Octave

Ask your singers to actually show you the length of their vocal folds (1/2 inch–3/4 inch) with their fingers. Then you demonstrate what the difference looks like in the folds when singing an octave leap. There is no visible change noticeable to the eye.

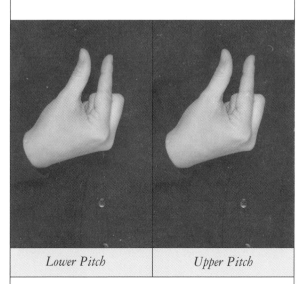

| *Lower Pitch* | *Upper Pitch* |

yo   ho

Music Exercise 7: Singing Octaves

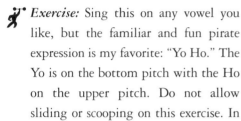

🏃 *Exercise:* Sing this on any vowel you like, but the familiar and fun pirate expression is my favorite: "Yo Ho." The Yo is on the bottom pitch with the Ho on the upper pitch. Do not allow sliding or scooping on this exercise. In every case, try to make the upper pitch resemble the lower one as much as possible to demonstrate the similarity in how they are made. The object of this exercise is to show the students they need not be afraid of high notes or leaps to high notes. The actual vocal muscles move only the slightest bit. The brain tells them how far to stretch. Their only task is to listen, and supply enough breath and relaxation for the folds to do the work. (See Music Exercise 7.)

16. The Inner Tube Octave

Once you have done the above, ask the singers to put their hands back on their inner tube. Then we are going to sing the same octave leap. First, ask them to do it with no inward movement of the inner tube. You will be surprised how difficult this is. But the octaves will soon float, isolating the actual tiny movement of the vocal fold. Then, ask them to sing the same octave with a dramatic pulling in of the abdominal muscles on the high note. They will automatically feel that the vocal folds have no choice but to immediately act as a valve, thickening and responding to the sudden upward flow of breath by tensing.

Inner Tube Octave

17. The Bowling Octave – Sha!

Using the same octave jump, have the singers spread out far enough to pretend they are actually bowling. This can be with or without the preparatory steps (depending on your space). "A" is the prep that goes with the arm windup, "Ha" is sung just as you go down to release the ball (or the tone). This must be done with reckless abandon in order to work.

Bowling

18. Something Stuck on My Finger Octave

Of course you know by now that the interval does not have to be an octave, but any leap upward. This one is fun and easy to do. Imagine you have something stuck to your finger…like, say, a wad of rubber cement or something like that. When you sing the lower note, your hand is somewhere around your face or higher. As you sing the upper note, you try to flick that stuck substance to the ground. You'll be amazed at how relaxed and easy the upper pitch will be.

19. Falling on a Bean-Bag Chair Octave

Now, that is a description, isn't it? But my teacher in Austria had me do just that. Going for the high note while falling into a soft chair teaches you all manner of things about yourself and the muscular tension you attach to high notes. This can be done with choir chairs—you just have to be more careful. Standing for the lower pitch, the singer drops into the chair for the upper pitch. When doing an exercise like this one, the singer will automatically notice how much attention, and thus tension, they are attributing to the laryngeal area instead of focusing on the actual movement of the exercise. The goal is to take focus away from the vocal mechanism.

20. Two by Two Octave

Have the chorus number off 1–2, 1–2 across each row as they did in earlier exercises. This time the "ones" are going to sing the octave exercise. The "twos" are going to take the hands of the "ones" at their sides. When the "ones" sing the upper octave, the "twos" pull down (not back, but straight down) to give the "ones" that feeling of the upper octave being down, not up. About-face. Repeat.

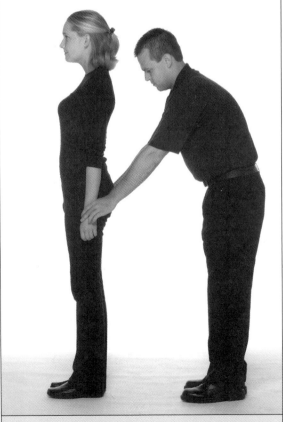

2 x 2

21. Buckets of Cement

Once they have experienced the feeling of actually having someone pull down on their hands as they leap to the upper octave, ask them to simply pretend they have buckets of cement in their hands, down at their sides. On the lower octave, the buckets have only five pounds of cement in them. But on the higher octave, the buckets miraculously and instantly weigh 100 pounds!!

22. To staccato or Not

Many choral conductors and voice teachers hammer away at staccato exercises, much to the detriment of the fragile balance of the onset of tone. Light staccato is excellent for both flexibility of the breathing mechanism and for coordination of the attack. However, when staccato is used at forte or louder, it becomes both tiring on the vocal folds and negative reinforcement in the area of breathing. Harsh staccato with dramatic movement in the abdominal muscles is what forces the vocal folds to react to the extra breath pressure by tensing. This does not allow the folds to function in a free manner (See Fountain of Youth, Chapter 3, Exercise 7; Music Exercise 8.)

One more word here. We already know how to jerk in the abdomen. We use this motion all the time for many involuntary body

ha ha ha ha ha ha ha ha   ha ha ha ha ha ha ha ha   ha

Music Exercise 8: Bouncing (Advanced Choir: Triplets)

functions: coughing; clearing our throats; yelling at football games; getting sick afterwards. We do not automatically know how to coordinate a light abdominal motion with the onset of tone nor the steady support system involved in creating freedom. Considering the fact that we already have daily experience with the dramatic abdominal jerk and the vocal fold tension that accompanies it, it stands to reason that all or most staccato exercises should be done lightly. Also fairly obvious is that all choirs can sing loud. Training them to sing softly is much more challenging. Light staccato is a great start.

23. Personal Neck Brace

The palms of your hands are very sensitive. Much like you have asked your singers to put their hands on the sides of their faces in "The Scream," this time the palms go on the sides of the neck as they sing. Asking them to rest their chin lightly on the hands is also fine. This is reinforcement of relaxation of everything above the larynx while singing.

Personal Neck Brace

Registers:
head, chest,
shoulders, knees
and toes

REGISTERS

Head, Chest, Shoulders, Knees and Toes

This is always one of the most difficult topics to discuss. It seems the description always lies somewhere between much too simple and much too complex. I have found that avoiding the terms "head and chest voice" helps me in teaching my singers. They are now totally on board with "heavy mechanism" and "light mechanism." It may not be easy for you to make this change, but I promise it is worth it. There is a long tradition working against you, though; even further back than your kindergarten teacher. The first traceable mention of head and chest was in the 1300s when Jerome of Moravia distinguished between what he heard as vox pectoris (chest voice) and vox capitis (head voice). What was he thinking?

One of the most famous singing teachers of all times and the inventor of the laryngeal mirror, Manuel Garcia II, put forth a definition of "registers" that is still very accurate today. It is "a serious of homogeneous sounds produced by one mechanism, differing essentially from another series of equally homogenous sounds produced by another mechanism."

Registration refers to the process of using and combining registers to achieve artistic singing in certain parts of the range (or for each note). Everyone has a heavy mechanism and a light mechanism and most of us are striving to blend the two. All men have falsetto (regardless of what they say).

The real issue is whether a singer demonstrates static adjustment of the vocal folds or has learned dynamic adjustment of the musculature.

Static adjustment results in completely separate timbre from one set of notes to the next. It also results in breaks, cracks, black holes in the range, and the pesky passagio pothole to be discussed. These faults comes from a lack of smooth transition through the range, ascending or descending. Static adjustment does, however, make decent money for yodelers.

Dynamic adjustment is just the opposite. When singing a scale in either direction, the voice should adjust itself naturally for the changing of pitch, to a point where there are no abrupt changes in tone (or registers).

Perfect dynamic adjustment is perhaps our Holy Grail. Most singers, especially amateurs, have not mastered this technique and therefore have areas in their voices where there are fairly drastic changes in timbre and amplitude. I keep telling them there are no such things as "breaks." I don't think they really believe me, though.

This natural tug of war within the musculature of the larynx can be trained, just as any other muscle adjustment in the body. Much of the problem is psychological rather than physical and when told what to do and how to do it, the results are sometimes quite dramatic. As you know, much of the problem is not on the note that cracks or breaks, but the notes surrounding that area.

Vowels Make the Difference

Do the vowels I chose for warm-ups have anything to do with the registers? And do they really make a difference in transferring the warm-ups to the music? Oh, my goodness. ABSOLUTELY!!!

I believe this may be one of the biggest problems teachers and conductors create in the warming up of their choruses. And that problem is to default to [a] for every vocalise. How many times have I heard conductors begin warm-ups with the [a] vowel in the upper registers, mostly singing forte, and then they wonder why their chorus screams when it gets to the repertoire? Then they wonder why they can't understand the essence of singing piano in the upper ranges? Well, if I had a dollar for every time I have heard this, I could forego royalties on this book you have just bought. The vowels you choose have a dramatic effect on the actual makeup of the vocal folds.

The scientific data behind the way vowels affect the actual vocal folds is there for you to read. Formants give each particular vowel its color and timbre. Formants, for our discussion here, are described as frequencies in the overtone series in which acoustic energy is enhanced. The vowels we sing change the tension and texture of the folds, in collaboration with the production of that vowel.

Here is the problem. The [a] vowel has clustered formants and because of this it is the most difficult vowel to sing consistently throughout the range. The vocal folds, responding to the vowel you have chosen, are automatically thicker on the [a] vowel, causing it to be heavier. It is the most difficult vowel to adjust to light mechanism.

The [i] vowel and its neighbors are tense and thinner at the vocal-fold level and tend to automatically have "ring" (and some tension) in them. The vowels [o] and [u] make the vocal folds lax and the sound more round with less "ring". In general, [u] will achieve the lightest adjustment, [a] will achieve the heaviest, and [i] the most tense with the most ring.

So, you will have to make a <u>conscious decision</u> of what you are trying to achieve with your chorus when you select the vowels for each exercise. This is not to be taken lightly and, I repeat, [a] should not automatically be your default every time just because you have not thought this through. If anything, I default to [u] or [o] in the upper range, as you will see later in some of the exercises.

NOW THE FUN BEGINS

1. NASCAR

This is one of the simplest ways to help everyone relate registers to something in their own lives. Think of the gears on the car. In fact, in the privacy of your office or home, make the noise you used to make as a kid when you were mimicking a race car changing gears. You got it. First gear = heavy mechanism. Each gear higher is a higher register. Then you downshift back into heavy mechanism as the car slows.

2. Pesky Passagio Pothole

As you know, the "passaggio" is literally the passage between registers. It is like a pothole in the middle of the vocal range. Ignoring the pothole by driving around and pretending it is not there is not an appropriate solution, but it is done every single day. Facing the pothole head-on seems to be the best approach. If you had an issue with a malfunction of any other muscle in your body, you would find exercises to strengthen that area. The same applies to the

muscle adjustment required here. We simply need to address the issue directly. One of the most logical ways is to increase the focus of your work on things such as the portamento, siren, etc., paying close attention to the dynamic adjustment. Much has been written about only using descending exercises to bring the head voice down. This is a worthy admonition. However, it has to work the other way as well. In the following exercise (#9), the pyramid of heavy(low) light (high) mechanism is reinforced by the vowels used.

Exercise: The first three-note scale is sung in a full-voiced [a], decrescendo on the final 1, before a perfect slide (no yodel or gaps) up to the octave on [u] then down, migrating through [o] and back to [a] on the bottom. (See Music Exercise 9.)

3. Messa di Voce Magic

The actual translation of this Italian term is "mass of the voice" or "setting up the voice." This one exercise has gotten more attention through the years than just about any other. In

Music Exercise 9: The Slide Is the Most Important

[a]————   [u]————   [o]————   [a]

Music Exercise 10: Messa di Voce

truth, there is probably no single exercise that, if done properly and developed throughout the range, can build a voice as well as this one. It is one you must continue to develop in your chorus. I have my accompanist give me a chord and allow the singers to choose the note they like the best (never hurts to give them just the slightest notion that they are in control!). We start with a beautiful, relaxed pianissimo [a].

You will notice, most likely, that the crescendo is fairly smooth, providing a nice, even side to the dynamic pyramid. On the decrescendo, however, you will notice stair steps of dynamics, rather than a smooth slide down the other side of the pyramid. That is static adjustment of the vocal folds. In addition to the unevenness of the decrescendo, the singers' automatic response to the decrescendo is to close the throat as well. This makes a final sound that has no relation to the sound with which the chorus started.

There are several instructions to the chorus that will begin to fix both of these issues. The yawn and sigh enter here. As the chorus attempts the decrescendo, coach them to keep the air flowing at a steady pace, never cutting back on it. At the same time, they need to be conscious of the continual yawn throughout the decrescendo. Yes, it is a lot to think about, but will hugely affect your chorus' sound and artistry. (See Music Exercise 10.)

4. Echo Messa di Voce

Another exercise to assist in the decrescendo is the echo.

Exercise: Give the singers a feel for what the decrescendo feels like. Ask them to sing a forte "Hey" as if they were standing at the edge of a huge cavern or in the Swiss Alps, with an echo coming back at them. The echo comes back in an evenly spaced dynamic decrescendo. They will sing five "hey's" in perfect diminuendo. Then take the echo away and ask them to do that decrescendo on a simple [a].

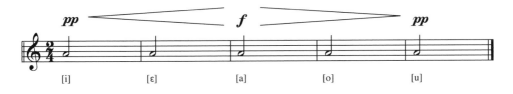

Music Exercise 11: Vowels Series Encouraging Messa di Voce

5. Messa di Voce with Vowels

The previous exercises give your singers the opportunity to hone their crescendo/decrescendo skills on the [a] vowel. This is a great exercise and one that should be in every conductor's bag of tricks.

In line with the theory that vowels do impact the vocal-folds, the series of vowels shown above (#11) will lead your singers from a thinner vocal-fold production on the beginning pianissimo, to the thicker vowel for the forte, then back to lax for the final pianissimo. (See Music Exercise 11.)

6. Good Tension/Bad Tension

How does a sound go from piano to forte? Ask this of your singers and you will get blank stares and then a host of answers – like the mouth, the

jaw, the diaphragm, air, etc. Then have them do the messa di voce again. When they do this and begin to actually think about what makes a sound crescendo, they realize that it is indeed two things at once: increased air and increased tension (of the good sort) in the vocal folds. Any imbalance in this delicate adjustment will cause the tone to either become tight or breathy. Ask them to do that as well just to feel the difference. If they experience what it feels like to do it wrong, they are less likely to repeat it.

7. Denial

Denial is not just a river in Egypt.
Too many singers are in denial that there are such things as register problems in their voices. In many ways, the messa di voce does wonders to help singers understand dynamics. This exercise highlights for them the difference in heavy, mixed, and light mechanism. It is also

Music Exercise 12: Mixing Mechanisms.

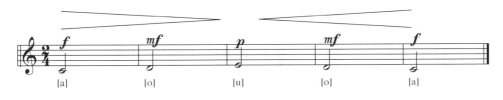

one that will help them achieve that scary feat of letting go of weight or tension in an ascending direction. Actually quite simple, it should be done in the sequence of the vowels given. These vowels will do some of the work automatically: we use [a] for heavy mechanism; [o] for mixed; and [u] for light mechanism. The exercise moves up and down by half steps, focusing on whatever troubled area your singers may have. Altos begin on middle C and work up perhaps a fourth. Sopranos can work their pesky pothole that occurs, perhaps beginning with F, a fourth above middle C and going up a fourth as well. (See Music Exercise 12.)

Once the concept has been understood completely on the above vowels, try it on [a] throughout. This is very difficult to do in the beginning, but, like the messa di voce, will do wonders.

8. Static Cling

In the untrained or out of practice voice, the real issue is static adjustment of the musculature in the larynx. A smooth transition from one series of notes to the next is difficult because of lack of understanding and lack of attention to the issue of registers. Static adjustment of the registers is quite simple to demonstrate. Sing a scale from a very low pitch, keeping the heavy mechanism fully "engaged," until there is no choice but to make a radical adjustment in order to move any higher in the scale. This may result in cracking or at the very least a huge shift in tone quality.

This negative modeling is best done on an [a] all the way up. I like to demonstrate this by forming what would be a vocal fold with bundles of muscles for heavy mechanism. As I begin up the scale, I keep all of the fingers pulling on each other until my voice breaks and all of the fingers let go: static adjustment.

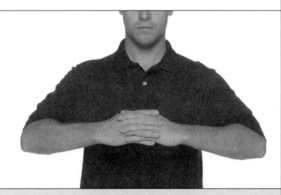

Heavy Mechanism

Light Mechanism

| *Forte Bottom* | *Piano Top* |

Then I demonstrate dynamic adjustment by beginning the same way, but as I ascend and let weight or thickness off the folds by an even decrescendo toward the top, I allow one finger at a time to drop as the folds thin out leaving only the pinky finger vibrating in the top.

As I go back down the scale, I add the fingers back one at a time as the muscle mass returns to the folds.

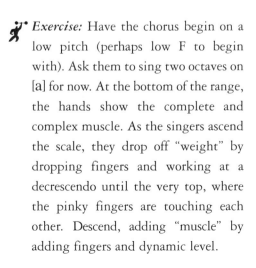

Exercise: Have the chorus begin on a low pitch (perhaps low F to begin with). Ask them to sing two octaves on [a] for now. At the bottom of the range, the hands show the complete and complex muscle. As the singers ascend the scale, they drop off "weight" by dropping fingers and working at a decrescendo until the very top, where the pinky fingers are touching each other. Descend, adding "muscle" by adding fingers and dynamic level.

9. $10,000 Pyramid

On the game show, "$10,000 Pyramid," the prize was given to the person who began at the bottom rung and worked his/her way to the top. Only when this was accomplished, in that order, was the game won. Much can be said about the correlation of building the voice and the choir. Beginning work in the top of the voice is a very dangerous way to go about it. Building a good foundation and understanding of the vocal mechanism in the bottom range before extending it upward is a much more logical approach. There is a reason pyramids are broader at the bottom than at the top.

Exercise: Ask the singers to sing an ascending octave scale (or exercise of your choice). On the bottom, their hands are as in the first picture and they are singing the [a] vowel forte. As they ascend, the hands move to the up and down position and they migrate the vowel to [u] as they decrescendo. Then back down, back to [a] and back to forte and back to the first hand position. This exercise helps them understand the pyramid shape of vocal registers. You can certainly have them reverse the pyramid to make it upside down to show them how unnatural piano in the bottom and forte in the top is when building their voices (and your choir).

10. Boo

This is the best range extension exercise I know, taught to me by my wonderful voice teacher at the Mozarteum in Salzburg. It is just incredible and choirs love to do it (once they get used to it). First of all, it gets their minds off singing and makes it a game. Once they have accepted the fact that most of what they do is listen for the pitch, get tension out of the way, and supply air to the instrument, this exercise becomes great fun.

Exercise: Have the chorus turn a quarter turn toward the center, elbows up, fingers even with eyeballs, pointing toward each other in front of eyes. A pitch is played and the singers move the fingers toward each other, trying to surprise themselves as they sing. The exercise is 8–5–3–1 with a boo on 8 and 3 (#15). The accompanist

Hands in Front of Eyes

Fingers Past Eyes

moves up by 1/2 steps. Do not allow any searching for pitch, or any scooping. The singers will be forced to "let go" of the weight in their voices as they ascend. Actually, they won't even

Boo_____   boo_____

Music Exercise 13: Finding the Perfect Registration...Let Off the Muscle as You Ascend. Keep Going!

be thinking of it, because it is so much fun. When you have finished, tell them how high they just sang with no tension and no muscle. They will be astounded. When an entrance in a piece of music is high and they are afraid of it, take this exercise right to it. Start about a fourth below the entering pitch in the music and work up to it on "Boo." When they get to the actual pitch, tell them that is where that entrance should lie in their voices. They will get it. (See Music Exercise 13.)

Registers or Registration

The last two exercises bring up the topic of registration. The discussion of how many registers there are is one that can and does fill books. Is there one? Are there three? Is every note in a singer's range its own register? Perhaps there are really none. I believe that when your singers do the previous exercise, they are likely to find an adjustment of the vocal folds that is ideal for each and every pitch. When they truly "let go" of the weight

as they ascend the scale, each pitch falls into place in a pyramid shape. The singer will feel the comfort of that adjustment. Of course, it is up to the singer to adjust the level for singing that is louder or softer than the mid-line. However, in repertoire, when any voice part begins in the upper range and the singers tend to grab, scream or simply get frightened, go back and do the "Boo" exercise until they reach the pitch in the music. Remind them of how good that feels and that they should try to reproduce that feeling when approaching that particular entrance. Of course, getting quickly past any consonants will also help.

11. What Goes Up, Must Go Down

I ask my singers to "float down" in the range. The tendency in most singers is to "mash" down on the lower notes, thinking that will help them project. This does not work. We spent a lot of time working on the downward motion required for the high notes. Now we take a little time to talk about range enhancement on the low end. The range cannot be extended, but the range that is there can certainly be developed.

Music Exercise 14: Floating Down

 Exercise: As the singers descend on the vowels shown in musical exercise 14, ask them to allow their hand to float from around the face level up to the sky on the bottom. Not only will this encourage the use of air throughout the exercise, but it also encourages the singers to keep the soft palate in the arched position. Allow this for fuller resonance rather than getting lazy and allowing the palate to sag, cutting off much of the richness of the overtone series.

Float Down

Top of Scale

12. Portamento

"The best thing in the world." Many have extolled the virtue of the portamento or the descending slide. Actually, sliding in either direction is very good for the vocal folds. Take your silly putty as an example. When warming it up, you don't pull it in jerky motions (approximating a scale passage or arpeggios) but rather in smooth strokes with

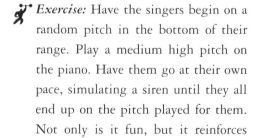

Music Exercise 15: Ear-Training Slide

no jerking. This is what a portamento will do for your folds. You can choose the intervals to help you in repertoire or ear training. (See Music Exercise #15.)

13. Siren

The opposite of the portamento, this is an ascending exercise not unlike the NASCAR gears. The object is the sliding to warm up the folds. The side result is that the singers get preoccupied with the siren and forget that there are such things as registers or tension while ascending.

Exercise: Have the singers begin on a random pitch in the bottom of their range. Play a medium high pitch on the piano. Have them go at their own pace, simulating a siren until they all end up on the pitch played for them. Not only is it fun, but it reinforces several concepts at once.

14. Tessy Tura

No, it is not one of your sopranos. "Tessitura" has been defined in several ways. One definition is the area of the range in which your singers are most comfortable singing. A quick way to find it is to determine the range of the entire piece (or a single page). Find the average pitch, and you have the tessitura. The pitch will actually give you a idea of where the voice parts lie. The range of a piece is fairly irrelevant when compared to the tessitura. A piece that has an octave range in a given part may look completely do-able. However, if the average pitch lies at the very top of that octave, it may tire your singers because of the high tessitura. The reverse is also true. You, as a conductor, need to be sensitive to this as you select music and then as you deal with the music you have chosen.

One very effective way to allow singers some autonomy is to let them choose the pitch in the chord you play for chordal exercises. I find this almost always works out terrifically. They won't always choose the same note in the chord, which will encourage them to listen as well.

Exercise: Give the chorus a chord of your choice. Ask them to pick a note. Have them sing a series of vowels on the pitches they have chosen. Then, ask them to switch notes! This helps get them out of the normal rut each of the parts usually fall in and will help tuning as well.

15. Bumble Bee

This exercise used earlier to work on steady breath flow over the vocal folds, can now be used to even out the registers. Singers who may have psychological issues with changing registers or high notes will find those issues disappear when they focus on keeping their lips buzzing. This relaxed airflow and lack of tension in the larynx allows the folds to adjust much easier than when singing vowels or repertoire.

 Exercise: Use the siren on an 8- or 9-note scale to demonstrate the ease of register transition.

CHAPTER 6

Resonators:
woofers and tweeters

RESONATORS

Woofers and Tweeters

> *"There is nothing in the human mechanism by which a singer can place, focus, or throw the sound anywhere."*

James C. McKinney

So, if we can't "place" or "focus" a tone, then what do we do? Well, the answer is "resonator adjustment." It is a logical way to instruct your singers to get the sound you want. Instrumentalists have resonance chambers that are fixed, and pitch is adjustable with valves or frets. Not so with singers. Resonator adjustment does not have to be as mysterious as we vocal folks have made it through the years.

Here are the possible resonators (from bottom to top):
Chest; Tracheal tree; Larynx; Pharynx; Mouth; Nose; Sinuses; THE WORLD.

Improbable resonators:
Chest (forced resonance) - too much covering of skin, fat, muscle.
Tracheal tree, larynx - not controllable or adjustable.
Sinuses – not adjustable and often clogged.

Probable resonators remaining:
Nose; Mouth; Pharynx; THE WORLD…

The three basic resonators that we can control are the throat (pharynx), the mouth and the nose. That makes it fairly simple. And in a moment, we will actually take the nose out of the equation for all practical purposes.

And why THE WORLD, you say? Because it is true. When your chorus performs in various rehearsal or concert venues, that space then becomes their final and largest resonator. A conscious effort must be made on your part to fill that space with sound as with any of the resonators inside the body. The goal is to fill the space, not peel the paint off the back wall (a concept often used in earlier years).

1. Get Rid of the Nose

Ask your singers to make a very nasal sound (you can use Randy Travis or Willie Nelson as examples) on a dull vowel such as "uh." As they hold the sound, they should pinch their nose shut and let go several times. They will hear and feel definite changes in the timbre. Now, ask them to apply the dynamic duo of "yawn and sigh" to the tone in their most beautiful "pear-shaped" tone (more on the pear later). Then, have them pinch and release their noses. Ah! Who knew? No change.

That's the secret. When the throat is open fully, the soft palate cuts off access to the nose. The only time we really use the nose to any extent is in French nasals.

Close Nose

Open Nose

2. Palate Play (French Nasals)

There is a simple way to practice the actual raising and lowering of the soft palate as an exercise. Have your singers look in the mirror at home while stretching their mouth as wide as possible. With good lighting, the singers will be able to watch the uvula disappear as the soft palate rises.

Exercise: While singing a beautiful [o], create a nice yawn and round sound. Ask the singers to change that [o] to the French nasal [õ] and then back to the open-throated [o]. This allows them the opportunity to isolate and exercise the raising and lowering of the soft palate. Repeat on the other three French nasals.

[æ] – [ɛ̃]

[ɔ] – [ã]

[ʌ] – [œ̃]

3. Nose Fun

Now that you have done the soft palate exercise, try this just for fun. Ask the singers if they think they can hum and hold their nose. Most will definitely think they can. Surprise!

Options Narrowed

Now the usable resonators are down to two: Mouth and Throat. These are the two "rooms" that determine the color of the tone.

Throat

The ceiling of the throat (pharynx) is the soft palate, which can be raised.

The floor to the throat is the larynx, which can be lowered.

The walls of the room can also be widened with conscious stretching of the throat.

The orifice is large and fleshy, and enhances the fundamental and lower overtones.

Mouth

The roof of the mouth is the hard palate. It can't be moved.

The floor is the tongue. It can be moved by relaxation.

The orifice is small, with hard surfaces, including the teeth, and encourages higher overtones and ring.

4. Mouth Floor

We have discussed the ceiling of the pharynx (soft palate) and the floor to the pharynx (larynx). These allow the pharynx to expand. But the floor of the mouth is equally important. It should be relaxed and out of the way and there are several ways to do this. Perhaps the easiest way for your singers to self-judge if they are letting the tongue get in their way is to use their pencil or pen as a guide.

On a simple [a] vowel, have them rest their pencil gently on their tongue that is relaxed and lying on the base of the mouth. Sing a simple scale. They will feel the pencil move as tension creeps in. No more needs to be said. Unless, of course, you come from the old school that liked to pass out squares of gauze and asked them to grab their tongues and pull them out as they sing. Ouch.

Don't Try This

Woofers and Tweeters

Those of us who are older remember when the fairly ornate front panels to our bulky stereo speakers would fall off and reveal the magic: woofers (big speakers) and tweeters (small speakers). Interestingly enough, today our kids get even better sound with speakers the size of a dime. But they still understand woofers and tweeters. The woofers are the things that make the car thump to the rhythm of the music; the tweeters are the things that help them understand talk radio (or rap). Everyone understands adjusting the "tone" knob on their radio or stereo. As conductors or vocal coaches, this is what we do in regards to resonator adjustment. It is really the true indicator of tonal preferences of the conductor more than any one thing.

5. Baby Bird or Swan?

Of all the exercises in this book, this one will probably make the most light bulbs go off for your singers. It is the simplest way to demonstrate the "resonator adjustment" from tweeter to woofer and back again.

🏃 *Exercise:* Select a medium pitch. Place your finger at the side of your face and in front of your mouth (see first figure). Make the brightest, most forward, white toothy [a] you can make. It should be all tweeter. Staying as true to the [a] vowel as you can, move the finger back along the side of the face to just behind the ear (see second figure). As the finger moves, the space moves, mirroring the placement of the finger. Midpoint should be a well balanced sound and as

it moves back, make as dark and even swallowed sound as you can (woofer). Reverse the direction and move it back to the front. If you want, you can use the beak of a baby bird for the tweeter and move it back to the hand position we use when making a shadow puppet of a swan.

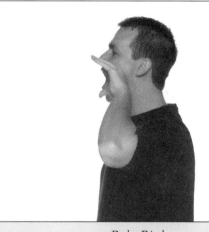

Baby Bird

Swan

6. Adjusting the Tone Knob

When the full chorus is singing, they can't always understand or hear what you are trying to achieve. Divide the chorus in half. Have one half do the exercise while the other half listens. Ask the nonsinging half to raise their hands when the sound is pleasing to them and drop their hands when it is no longer pleasing. Swap the groups. They will have a blast and learn about simply adjusting the resonators to adjust their tone knob. Have them all do it and then stop them when YOU like the tone of the entire group. Whether we consciously think of it or not, we have a favorite resonator adjustment. That is why you hear choirs that are decidedly "dark" or "bright." It is because the conductor consciously or subconsciously prefers that color and has taught it to his/her chorus. Other ways that achieve this same effect will be discussed later.

Treble knob–toward talk radio. This moves the voice toward the proverbial "ring" at 2800–3200 Hz., and is what gives the voice projection or "carrying power" over an orchestra. It can also give that one soprano or tenor the ability to ruin everything you have worked toward in choral rehearsals! The pathway to developing this lies in things like humming, [ŋ], etc.

Bass knob–toward thumping bass. Turning up the bass knob encourages the fundamental and the lower overtones. This sound can become colorless if too many of the upper overtones are discouraged by dampening them in the soft cavern of the pharynx. All yawn - type exercises encourage this.

7. Elastic Band

This is the most valuable tool you can purchase for almost no money. Go to the fabric store or Wal-Mart (or send "your people"). Purchase several yards of 1-inch wide elastic, and cut them in 8-inch lengths. Give everyone in your chorus this lovely party favor. You will never be sorry they have this in their possession. The elastic is useful for helping the singers feel the different adjustment of the resonators. For example, in the first picture, the elastic band is held in front of the face, resulting in a spread, white, "blatty" sound. When the singers move the band back toward the ear and match the space to the position of the band, the sound will change dramatically. The elastic band can be stretched to simulate the stretch of the mouth or the pharynx, depending on where it is placed. As a bonus, tell them to hold the elastic in front of their bodies to demonstrate the stretch of the sound horizontally rather than vertically.

Front Space

8. Look, Ma: One Hand

With only one hand, your chorus can visualize the shape you want the sound to be. Ask them to sing a chord on an [a] vowel. Each singer places his/her hand vertically in front of their face and mimics the shape of the hand, singing nice tall vowels with relaxed jaw, vertical stretch in the pharynx, and even a feeling of support in the entire body.

Back Space

Vertical

9. Look, Ma: Wrong Way

Now ask the chorus to sing the same chord on the same vowel but change the hand position to horizontal, and mimic the shape of what they are seeing in front of them. The vowels will be sideways, spread, and there is also no

There is no sound that is horizontally conceived that is beautiful.

indication of support from below the chest. From then on, that hand signal from you should tell them all they need to know about what kind of sound you want from them.

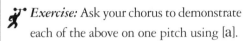
Horizontal

10. Three Bears of Space

Really nothing to do with bears at all, but three options, the third of which is "just right." When singing any vowel, you have three options:

1. Vowel in the front, space in the front. This is the bright, forward sound with no "roundness."
   "This sound is too bright."
2. Vowel in the back, space in the back. This is the dark, woofy sound that has no

understandability.
"This sound is too dark."

3. Vowel in the front, space in the back. This one is just right and will allow for beautiful round singing plus the brightness that will make the sound balanced.
   "This sound is just right."

Exercise: Ask your chorus to demonstrate each of the above on one pitch using [a].

11. Pear-shaped Tone

But where is the pear? It is one of those ironies of life that we have grown up extolling the "pear-shaped" tone and never really thinking about where the pear is supposed to go. I have no doubt it conjures up some open throat ideal in a beginning singer just by virtue of the image of forcing a whole pear inside one's mouth. But I feel quite certain there is some doubt about positioning! We did have some fun actually placing the pear. You have read enough in this book to know that my ideal position is with the large end of the pear in the pharynx and the small end in the mouth. Others obviously disagree by the sound of their choirs. The second choice is the reverse of the pear. The last one is probably not even an option, but who ever heard of "The Two Pears."

Too Bright

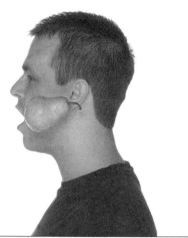

Too Dark

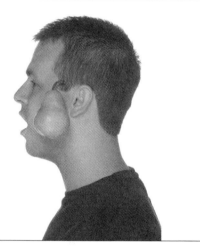

Just Right

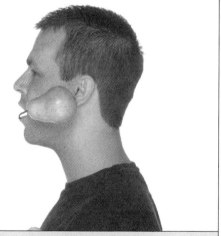

The Three Pears

12. Chiaroscura

Chiaro–light; scuro–dark
This term is used in balancing the resonators with bright and dark, front and back. Is it too dark? Is it too bright? Are they singing in the throat? Are they singing in the mask? It is always the issue of balance of the light and the dark, the mouthy and the throaty. There are several exercises to help with this. One, of course, is the baby bird vs. swan. But even more basic is the light hum that comes when something dawns on you and you say "hmmmm." It is a sound that is not too dark, not too bright, it's just right.

Exercise: Ask the singers to say "hmmmm" at a normal pitch level of speaking, and prolong it. Ask them to raise the pitch several times and then open to an [i] vowel on the same sigh feeling. Choose an [i] vowel from something you are singing and sing it as you did the "hmmm."

Sing - ah

Music Exercise 16: Ring

13. A Really Good Sing-ah

This is a great exercise to begin the sound in the "mask" with a resonant consonant [ŋ], which adds ring. Then open to a nice round, relaxed throat [a]. You can coach your singers to leave as much of the [ŋ] in the sound as is pleasing to your ear, or open the throat and raise the soft palate to your heart's (or ear's) delight. The "sing-ah" can also be swapped for "hung-ah." (See Music Exercise 16.)

14. Fish Lips

When all else fails in convincing your singers they are spreading their lips, try this. As you already know, with each note higher in the range a singer sings, they are naturally searching for more space for that tone to resonate. The temptation is to find that space in the front of the mouth, resulting in a spread tone quality.

🏃 *Exercise:* To help your singers feel the natural tendency for the lips to spread as they go higher, ask them to sing a passage of their music that takes them into the upper registers. First, have them do it while allowing their mouths to spread or lips to widen. Then ask them to do it with fish lips. It will be very uncomfortable at first, but soon they will begin to naturally avoid the spread of the mouth and lips and sail into the upper portions of their range.

Fish Lips

Music Exercise 17: A Fine Day

15. This Is a Fah Fah Fah-ine Day Today

The first "fah" (on the first 8) is sung with the resonators in a normal speech mode. The second is in a full-throated, round sound. The third is in an overdone darkened stretch of the pharynx and then down on "day today" in the balanced voice of the middle option. This will demonstrate for your singers the three possible throat positions and again point out the balance factor on the middle 8. It is possible that the 3rd "fah" will be the best of the lot. This is because many singers will not allow themselves to truly exaggerate the stretched throat to create the swallowed sound. (See Music Exercise 17.)

16. Horse Teeth

In my opinion, no good can come of this mouth shape except maybe eating corn on the cob through the knot hole in a fence.

Horse Teeth

Choral singing: eclectic blender

CHORAL SINGING

Eclectic Blender

Blend, you rascals!

Robert Shaw

Actually, Robert Shaw used this phrase and then went on to describe how useless such a request is. It is not the singer, but the conductor who has to be able to find out what's wrong. Perhaps the color is wrong, perhaps the vowel is wrong, perhaps the pitch is wrong. Blend is not the result of one thing or the other, but the combination of many things.

Choir: The Team Sport Where No One Loses

What is "blend" after all? As you have read throughout this entire book, it is about balance. It is about balance of color and timbre, first in each voice, and then in the combining of individual voices to make a balanced sound. It is about matching vowels. The singers need to know what the shapes are that you are wanting. And they need to look like they are all singing the same vowel. I am sure you have probably had photos taken of your chorus while singing and from the shapes of the mouths of your singers, they could all be singing a completely different song.

Blend is also about balance of the resonance each of the singers is providing. If you have an operatically trained singer on one end of the spectrum with ring for days and a complete novice with a breathy, unpleasant sound on the other end, your challenge is to bring the two together.

Your own concept of blend depends on the aural modeling you as a conductor and singer have adopted for yourself. Later in the book, you will be asked to collect five of your very favorite choral recordings. Once you listen to them back to back, you will hear the ideal sound you are working toward.

My own theory is this: when working with amateur singers (not students preparing for operatic careers), probably 80% of those singers can sing successfully in my chorus and use 100% of the individuality inherent in their voices. There may be 10% who need to use only 90% of the color and timbre they possess. The final 10% (if we are lucky enough to have such singers who really want to be a part of a choir) will have to adjust accordingly to the group. I don't think I have ever asked a singer to remove more than 25% of their individual vocal prowess. If I had, I am sure it would have been a first tenor.

There are conductors who want all of the singers to remove all of the individual color of their voices in order to achieve a unified sound. Surely those conductors are not still reading this book.

How many times have you said or heard, "I want you to sound like one voice." Countless times, no doubt. But did you ever tell your chorus which voice you want them to sound like? Probably not. Therefore, at least half of your singers assume you mean them! And that is going to make each of them sing louder to make sure theirs is the one you (and everyone else) hear!!! As mentioned earlier, aural modeling is really important.

1. One Voice

In my experience, it has been beneficial to find a voice in each section that you find most fits the color and style of the piece you are working on. This will not be the same singer for every piece.

Have that singer sing a phrase so everyone can hear. Then, add singers to that voice, encouraging them to listen as they join in so they do not radically change the combined sound and color of the original singer. If you do this in each section, you will then only have the task of combining the sections to come up with the "one voice" you were looking for. This exercise also goes along with the vocal seating exercise later in this book that is so helpful in matching voices or placing voices that complement each other.

2. Matching Vowels with Hand Motions

This has become one of my favorite warm-ups. I know many conductors have used this technique or a variation of it for a long time. Where it first started probably no one knows. I first saw it used by my friend Jo-Michael Scheibe. He gets my eternal thanks. I am sure it has morphed over the years since I learned it. It consists of the chorus singing the five pure vowels. They are [i] [ɛ] [a] [o] [u]. Have the pianist play a chord and allow the singers to choose their own pitch within that chord. This allows them to choose the tessitura that is comfortable to them since the exercise is about vowel color not range extension.

[i] – lower chin, round lips, pull the "ee" out of the crown of the head.

[ɛ] – bring the hand around in front of the face and down in an elongating gesture.

[a] – simply loosen the jaw, getting rid of tension, but not dropping it too dramatically.

[o] – "lasso" the lips for the "oh."

[u] - pull the "oo" out as if through a straw.

Once your singers have heard how beautiful the unified vowels are, they are then better equipped to hear when they are not! They will hear the dramatic difference in the tone when you have carefully created a basis for understanding of each of the pure vowels. From there, you once again get to begin to color.

[a]

[i]

[o]

[ε]

[u]

3. Two Finger [a]

In order for your chorus to begin to match vowels, they need to look as if they are singing the same vowels. Begin with the [a] vowel. Ask your singer to place two fingers turned vertically in their mouths while singing an [a] vowel. The jaw should not be dropped in an exaggerated manner, just relaxed. Normally, two fingers will be just right (three too many? one too few?).

Two Finger

4. One Finger [o]

Along with the simple [a] vowel fix, there is an easy fix for the [o] vowel as well. This is one of those vowels that we don't ordinarily use our lips to shape well. Ask your singers to sing an [o] vowel, forte, and in the upper range. When they think they are singing it, ask them to check by putting one finger in their mouth. Basically, their lips can wrap around the finger. If your singers can fit multiple fingers in their [o] vowel, it's not a pure [o].

One Finger

5. Meow

It's OK to be catty in slow motion. Whodathunk? When you slow "meow" down, it has all five vowels [i] [ɛ] [a] [o] [u] and begins with a wonderful long hum! How perfect is that? Use this word on one held note, allowing the singers to feel the shift of the vowels throughout the resonators.

6. Yawn and Sigh

"They're back!"

With each new concept, we come back to the basics. Hands on sides of face with a big, relaxed yawn and sigh. If your singers do not have their throats open, those with closed throats will stick out. If your singers are not using the same breath pacing, they will stick out. If, however, they are all incorporating the same amount of each, you are at least starting out ahead of the game.

7. Choral Pyramid

There are many kinds of voices built in many different ways for different styles of music. I have found that for most choral music, the most efficient way to build an individual voice is in the shape of a pyramid. When you encounter a voice that is an inverted pyramid, good luck incorporating that one into your choir. In the same manner, the chorus needs to be built from the bottom up, not the other way around. Sure it is tempting to build an SATB chorus on the sopranos or a TTBB chorus on the first tenors. They are the ones, after all, who view themselves not so much as a voice part but more a lifestyle. Even though they assume you are building your chorus on them—and you don't have to actually tell them otherwise—my recommendation is to begin with the foundation—which is the basses (or altos in an SSA choir). Everything is built from that foundation upward. When each voice is built in a pyramid shape, then the chorus can be

Music Exercise 18: Building Blocks

built on the same principle. One upside down voice can spoil the whole thing.

🏃 *Exercise:* As you do Music Exercise 18 or another series of notes, keep in mind the sound we are working for is one that has the lower voices providing the foundation of the chord with the higher voices being the icing on the cake.

8. Singing as a Unit

Your singers must feel the music with each other. I have no doubt you have done this often, but this is your reminder. Have your choruses stand in a circle and sing to each other. This has great effect and multiple benefits. They will not only be able to see each other, instead of just the backs of everyone's heads, but will hear things they haven't heard before, both good and bad.

9. A Tighter Unit

This time, have your singers close their eyes and sing a portion of what you are working on from memory, or something you already have memorized, with no direction from you. You just set the tempo. If you have taught them well, they will be flawless. If not, they will crash and burn. Both can be fun.

10. Pre-hearing

Earlier it was said you can only sing as beautiful a sound as you can hear. This is completely true. Too often, we begin a song and then try to fix it midstream.

🏃 *Exercise:* Choose any of your pieces. Ask your chorus to sing it without any preparation. Then, ask them to close their eyes for a moment and imagine how beautiful that sound could be and what they can do themselves to make it all it can be. You will be surprised. Perhaps they will make a sound even more beautiful than the one you had imagined!

11. Sensitive Text Delivery

This is one of the most crucial areas we have to deal with and it is amazing how many conductors don't even consider this. When we speak, we use accented and unaccented syllables naturally. When we sing, we forget the natural rise and fall and give equal weight and importance to every single syllable. It makes the text boring and even unintelligible at times. Of course, this is absolutely imperative when singing foreign languages.

🏃 *Exercise:* Take a song you are singing. Decide what the most important words in the phrase are, then the accented and unaccented syllables. Next, ask the chorus to sing only those words you have selected as important in communicating the text (no ifs, ands, or buts). This is much like singing "Row, row, row your boat" and leaving off the last word with each singing. You will be amazed, when you go back to singing the phrase, how beautiful it will be. Do the same kind of exercise with unaccented syllables.

12. Path to Legato

There is a fairly simple three step-path to beautiful legato singing. The first step is to sing the phrase or the piece on one vowel chosen by you. The second step is to sing the phrase or piece on the vowels as written, but with no consonants. This is a real brainteaser for your singers, but it will teach them so very much. When they drop the consonants, they realize immediately the importance of pure and matched vowels. You won't have to say much at all. They will hear what needs to be improved. The final step is to add the consonants back in as punctuation. This may seem like a long process to go through for every piece, but once your singers get the knack, they won't have to do it on every piece or every phrase.

Exercise: Take any phrase from your repertoire (or every single piece if you have the time).

1. Sing it on one vowel.
2. Sing it on the vowels written (no consonants).
3. Add the consonants back in as punctuation.

13. Tractor Pull

When your chorus is still not grasping the concept of legato, or especially the energy required to create motion within the phrases, this is the answer! Divide 1–2, 1–2. Have them face each other and take the wrist of the other singer. First, sing the phrase with no feeling for legato or energy. Now have them pull on each others' arms, trying to pull the other person off balance. As they sing, coach them to pull harder through the phrase. They will laugh and have a great time. When they are finished, have them turn back to you. From that moment forward, whenever you need them to focus on legato energy, you must simply make that gesture and they will snap right into it.

Tractor Pull

14. Matched Pearls

Whatever exercise I am asking my singers to sing, I remind them that we are attempting to achieve a string of matched pearls. This means that every single tone in the exercise needs to have matched tone color, breath pacing, and most importantly, vibrato.

Exercise: Demonstrate for them a five note scale where one or more of the tones sounds like a puka shell instead of a pearl. They will get it. Again, not as easy as it sounds. With adults, you can use the analogy of sticking in a Baroque pearl. Kids understand puka much better.

15. Spin Cycle

Every tone should spin and shimmer, even the straight ones! But all too often our choruses slip into an over-produced, strident, "in your face" kind of tone. I often tell the chorus to caress me with the sound, don't assault me.

Exercise: Ask your chorus to sing a chord you give them or, more importantly, one from their repertoire. As they sing it, have them mash their finger into their palm, singing a straight, colorless, mashed sound. Now, ask them to repeat the chord making a sound that mimics the finger

gently caressing the palm and lightly vibrating or spinning. The result should be a wonderful, spinning, shimmering tone. Thanks to Geoffrey Paul Boers.

Mash

Caress

Hah   ah   ah   ah   ah   ah   ah   ah   ah   ah   ah   ah   ah

Music Exercise 19: Bouncing Epigastrium

16. Pulsating Legato

One of the questions I hear all the time is "How do I get my singers to find a vibrato?" The answer is pulsating legato. The first thing to get past is the psychological bias against vibrato in the first place, especially in young people. They equate vibrato with the soprano in the church choir who should have looked for other places of service about 20 years ago or the exaggerated opera singers in cartoons. In their experience, they don't have a great deal of aural modeling in their experience of good, natural vibrato. We know that vibrato is a natural occurrence in a free instrument. But getting the body and the breath and the vocal folds to all work at once is not automatic. The process is a three step one.

🏃 *Exercise:* Place a hand on the upper abdomen or epigastrium, just below where the ribs meet to check the flexibility of the breathing mechanism.

1. First, sing all notes on a light staccato. Epigastrium bouncing.

2. Next, sing the five notes on top staccato, descend legato, and then the five notes on the bottom staccato

3. Finally, all notes are sung quasi-legato but with pulsation on each note, just as on the first step, taking care that the epigastrium still bounces on every note.

17. More Vibrato

Repeat the exercise above. Once the final five pulses are finished, hold the final note for an extended time emphasizing the relaxed feeling of the vocal folds and breath. The held tone will begin to exhibit its own vibrato if the freedom of the mechanism is the focus.

> *"Sing like the train is leaving the station and you want to be on it!"*
>
> David Rayl

Music Exercise 20: Pyramid Alleluia

18. Alleluia

We have already ascertained that [a] in the bottom and [u] in the top reinforce the pyramid-building of heavy/light mechanism. This is an exercise the singers will all love, even if only because they are thinking "Hallelujah, surely we're almost done with warm-ups." (See Music Exercise 20.)

19. Bella Signora's Head

One of the most prominent vocal pedagogues of our time was John Large. He developed these two exercises to reinforce the teaching of smooth transitions from heavy (chest) to light (head) and light to heavy mechanism. The first exercise will help with the use of more open vowels on the bottom to the [o] vowel in the top, thus

relaxing and lightening the top. (See Music Exercise 21.)

20. Bella Signora's Chest

Dr. Large then reversed the exercise, allowing the singer to transit into the heavy mechanism in the bottom of the range, but using the [o] vowel to make sure it does not move into the "ugly" belting voice that might result on an [a]. (See Music Exercise 22.)

21. Vowel Migration Covering

The real issue here is that as one ascends in the range, the sound needs more space to resonate in order for the sound to remain beautiful.

Music Exercise 21: Lower Register

Music Exercise 22: Upper Register

Ask your singers to sing a pure [a] vowel, well balanced on an E major scale starting at the bottom and proceeding to the upper octave. If they do not change a single thing, the top note will most likely be "yelled," because no adjustment was made in the resonators to accommodate the higher pitch.

What to do? As I tell my singers, with each step higher you go in your range, the voice is trying to find a little more space in which to resonate. You have to provide that space somewhere. It is going to happen, period.

Some of the most common tools to help in this transition are vowel migration (you can call it "covering" if you wish, but that carries with it many bad connotations and potential pitfalls of allowing the vowel to drop back with the addition of space).

Many teachers encourage moving toward the closed partner of the open vowel being sung or simply moving toward the schwa.

[a] toward [ɔ] or [ʌ]
[ɛ] toward [e] or [i]
[ɔ] toward [o]
[o] toward [u]

22. The "Bad" Vowel

This is one of those really difficult issues that we all have to address. I find that it is really quite simple to explain, perhaps not so easy to accomplish.

Refer back to the Three Bears of Space discussion where the "just right" was the vowel in the front, space in the back and you have the answer. The [æ] vowel does not have to be changed to [a] in order to avoid it. Your chorus can make a beautiful [æ] as long as it is sung over an [a] space. When my chorus sang "Over the Rainbow," I literally died laughing when, for lack of knowing what to do with it, they sang, "if hoppy little blue birds fly beyond the rainbow…."

Music Exercise 23: Ear Training/Pyramid Building

23. Reed's 1-2-3

When you are tired of scales, this great exercise for ear training and for tuning chords in moving passages is quite easy and fun for the chorus. (See Music Exercise 23.)

24. Keeping the Space in Pianissimo

When we sing loud, we most often naturally have our throats expanded and the tone supported. Then, when we sing soft, we do two detrimental things: cut back on the air and close the space.

Exercise: We are going to use 1–5–1 on [a], first forte then piano. Chances are good they will automatically do the two things stated above. Then instruct them to concentrate very hard on making the piano portion just as full, open, and energized as the loud portion, by keeping the air moving and the space exactly as it was for the forte portion of the exercise. (See Music Exercise 24.)

25. Articulatin'

There are so many exercises for articulation out there. Many of them are very good and achieve the needed result of exercising consonants and making sure they fall together.

Music Exercise 24: Matching Piano to Forte

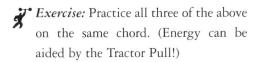*Exercise:* Use the rhythm of a familiar tune like "Row, Row, Row Your Boat." Whisper it staccato with consonants such as "ch" or "ts." You can also use a rhythmic portion of a piece in your current repertoire. The singers will automatically feel the importance of the consonants and the importance of coordinating them so they sound together.

26. No Sitting Still

A held note has to be going somewhere. Don't just let it sit there! How often do we say "Don't just let that note sit there" but then don't tell our singers what to do with it. Well, there are three choices. It can:

÷ Get louder
÷ Get softer
÷ Move forward with energy

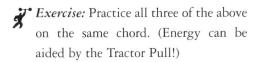*Exercise:* Practice all three of the above on the same chord. (Energy can be aided by the Tractor Pull!)

27. Beauty Box

This has become one of my favorites (and a favorite of my singers). Every person in your chorus (or solo singers for that matter) has a "beauty box" beyond which the sound is simply ugly (or "less beautiful," if your singers are sensitive). Each singer must know for themselves where the line of the beauty box is for them. They must stay behind that line at all times. If it is a song with a fortissimo ending, and you have them singing at the very top of their voices and then you ask for more, they should not give it. This has to do with your discipline in teaching them to not ever get right up to the line of their beauty box, and certainly not before the final beat of the final measure. Always save something.

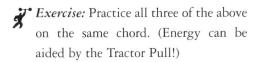*Exercise:* Choose the biggest final chord you have in your repertoire. Ask them to give their all. Then ask them to give a little more, just to where it starts to make your skin crawl a bit (in a bad way). Once they have experienced it, they won't want to do that again. Have them repeat it, singing the last note with 90% of what they have that

is still behind the beauty box. At the very last instant, ask them to give you the final 10%. Chill bumps are guaranteed.

28. Easy Chair Crescendo

Never let your singers hit the final note at the very top of their dynamic level and not have anywhere to go from there. Ask them to stand and put their hands on their rear ends. The knees need to be bent slightly and the pelvis tucked slightly and kept loose.

Have them sing the forte final note of a piece, not singing fortissimo (yet). Holding the note, ask them to push down with their hands and sink as if settling into a nice soft easy chair as they crescendo. Make sure they are not leaning back and tightening the abdominal muscles. The crescendo should be supported with the entire body. This will keep that final note from becoming screamy when produced from the chest up.

29. Why Breathe?

Singers should never take a breath because they need one. By that point, it is too late and the tone has suffered. You must allow them to only breathe for the expression in the phrase and for the meaning in the text.

This takes work from you to help them pace themselves through phrases.

Easy Chair

Exercise: Select a nice long phrase in a piece on which you are working. Ask them to sing the entire thing on one breath. Now, go back and give them a breath somewhere along the way that has to do with expressing the piece. They will notice a huge difference. This also applies to staggered breathing. The singers should never get to the end of a phrase and be starved for air.

30. Finger Cymbals

We need to find ways to keep our choruses, large and small, fully engaged in the pulse of whatever tempo you have set. Needless to say, they seldom rush, especially when music is new, but most often tend to drag until your arms are about to fall off. One word of caution I have learned from conducting adults. Do not snap your fingers at them! You cannot imagine how many "issues" are brought up subconsciously when you snap your fingers at them, whether they tell you about it or not.

It is just so much better to choose another method. I have three suggestions:

1. Use imaginary finger cymbals in one hand to keep the beat steady. Whenever the group gets out of sync, all I have to do is say "finger cymbals," and they fall right back into line.
2. Use one hand, crossed over the torso, to gently tap on your heart (or where we think the heart is). This helps internalize the beat.
3. Bounce on the balls of your feet when the piece is perky.

31. Singing Clusters

Those newfangled composers (who we adore) are writing some things that we aren't so used to. It is great to rehearse on some of these to get the chorus used to singing chordal structures that are not found in every anthem, Dick and Harry.

32. Eyebrows as a Tuning Tool

Once again, the "just say no" phrase works for this one. There is no question that I, as the conductor, use my eyebrows to communicate pitch issues with my singers. More often, I use one raised eyebrow to put fear into various singers or sections. When I raise both eyebrows, they know what the issue is, but I never ask them to raise theirs in order to sing in tune. I have done exhaustive research on this and have concluded that singers can sing really flat with their eyebrows hidden somewhere under their hairline! Not only does it not affect pitch, it looks really horrible. Tuning is obviously an ear thing, not an eyebrow thing. Work on ear training and tuning within various chordal structures. Much has been written on this and you can find books, videos, DVDs, etc. on tuning. My only warning is: don't use the eyebrows. P.S. I have also used the "thumb up" to try to communicate they needed to raise the pitch. They just thought I was giving them the "thumb's up" because they were doing such a good job!

Your conducting profile: know yourself first

YOUR CONDUCTING PROFILE

Know Yourself First

Before we launch into rehearsal technique and performance practice, let's look at you as a conductor/teacher. Richard Miller, in *On the Art of Singing*, lists pillars of performance success that are excellent for all of us who are conductors to review:

✢ Musicianship

✢ Understanding vocal technique

✢ Artistic imagination (musicality)

✢ Objectivity

✢ Perseverance

✢ Talent

✢ Business acumen

Exercise 1: Artistic Measure

My choral conducting students are given an exam that I believe would benefit you as well.

Rank yourself in each of the categories and then add the possible scores to see where you think you may fall as a successful artist. A score of 100 means you don't need to read this book!

	Your score
Musicianship (15)	_____
Understanding vocal technique (15)	_____
Artistic imagination (15)	_____
Objectivity (15)	_____
Perseverance (15)	_____
Talent (15)	_____
Business acumen (10)	_____

Your Total _____

This should give you a good idea of where you need to direct your focus on developing your conducting profile.

Attributes of a Good Instructor/Conductor

Since most of what we do is teach, this is a great measuring tool, also from Richard Miller.

1. Conductor/Singer Rapport

2. Diagnosis and Prescription

3. Specificity of Language

4. Efficient Use of Time

5. Measurable Results

The first is obvious, especially if you are conducting a volunteer chorus. Your singers won't return if there is no connection (and if it is not fun). The second is huge: know how to diagnose problems and learn how to fix them. The third is always a struggle, but if you can very carefully communicate with your singers what it is you want, and be consistent in that, you will succeed. Number 4 is enormous. Whether your chorus is volunteer or nonelective, you owe it to them not to waste any of their time. Efficient use of rehearsal time is crucial. Finally, for measurable results, there must be some way to know if they are actually "getting it" and moving toward the concepts you are sharing.

Exercise 2: Conducting Measure

Rank yourself in each of the following categories. Once again, this will help in your self-evaluation process. If you give yourself a 25, write your own book.

Conductor/Singer Rapport   _____

Diagnosis and Prescription   _____

Specificity of Language   _____

Efficient Use of Time   _____

Measurable Results   _____

Total   _____

Diagnosis

The first and largest portion of this book had to do with diagnosis and prescription. We are all very good at diagnosing problems when listening to other choruses. We are not always so objective about our own problems or, most importantly, how to go about fixing them.

Prescription Filled

Your chorus must be able to hear the difference when you diagnose a problem and prescribe a method for change. They must also be able to feel the difference in how they produce what you are asking them to change. At that point, they have three options:

1. Understand and like/accept the change you are requesting. This would be getting the prescription filled immediately.

2. Trust that you know what you're doing even if they don't like it or even understand it. Wait a few days to think about it before getting the prescription filled.

3. Find another chorus to sing in or other volunteer opportunity such as bowling or knitting.

4. Get a second opinion from another conductor.

Exercise 3: Practice Makes Perfect

This does not mean your chorus, but you. A difficult thing is to "practice" conducting alone. But it can be done. A mirror is a great thing for many reasons. Certainly every practice room in every school of music has one. You expect your singers to practice and they deserve the same thing from you. Conducting in a mirror, while frightening, will show you so much about what your singers are seeing, good and bad. When they frown at you or smile at you, they are your mirror! In addition, it will help you know if you are presenting them a model of relaxation and ease or one of tension and "over-conducting," which will only make them "over-sing."

James Jordan suggests conducting on one of those newfangled exercise balls and you know what? It works! The instructions from James are quite detailed. Bottom line is you sit on the exercise ball as you practice conducting. It gives you an incredible sense of balance and posture and stance. It helps center your conducting because if you get excited and do a gesture that is too far out of the box, you'll fall off the ball! "Yes, Virginia, conductors have beauty boxes, too!" And by using it for your conducting practice, you don't have to feel guilty about never having used it for exercising.

Exercise: Select a piece of music you are currently teaching and conduct it

in the mirror. It will frighten you at first, no doubt.

Exercise 4: "What They See Is What You Get!"

Never was there a more true statement than that from Rodney Eichenberger and Andre Thomas. You are sending your singers definite messages with your body language and your gestures. They are going to give you back exactly what they see. In addition, the audience does not need to see your every conducting move. You're not doing it for them after all. Every once in a while it is fun to really open up the conducting box to remind the audience who is in charge. More telling is a videotape of your front during a concert. You'll learn more from that humbling experience than just about anything you do.

Exercise: Videotape yourself conducting an actual concert. You need to have a videotape from the back of the hall focused on you, and another from somewhere in front so you can see yourself as your choir members see you.

TMI (Too Much Information)

There are many levels to learning a piece of music before you ever start. One of the most important things the conductor must do is to study the piece thoroughly.

Here are just some of the things you need to look at before your chorus ever sings a note:

✣ Key signature; key changes, meter; meter changes; dynamic peaks and valleys

✣ Horizontal movement: wide or difficult leaps; boring lines; mark beats when difficult

✣ Vertical relationships: interesting harmonic changes; find foundation; sing from bottom up

✣ Difficult entrances: what cues will they need? What vocal instruction? Where will they find pitch?

✣ Breathing issues: where are the breaths? Where are the long phrases with staggered breathing?

✣ Tone quality: what is required by the time period or the style of the piece

✣ Consonants: where are the difficult ones? Which ones might not be heard? Which ones may cause difficulty?

✣ The text: speak the text in rhythm; who wrote it? When and why?

How much of this information does your chorus really need?

After you have done all of this for yourself, decide how much you should share with your chorus.

I strongly urge using different color highlighters to mark the score so that when you are conducting through a piece, they jump out at you. Depending on how old you are, you may need a colorful reminder that the meter is changing or there is a subito piano or fermata.

Then decide how much of that information is important to have studied for yourself and how much your singers really need to know. Certainly the singers will be impressed by your studious care with the music. Then they will just want to sing. A good practice is to share bits with them as you go along in the rehearsal process. DON'T TALK TOO MUCH. I had a chorus member "share" with me that at a rehearsal at the beginning of a concert period, the conductor talked through the entire two and a half hour rehearsal about why she chose this piece or that and the background material on all of it. The chorus sat patiently with the music in their hands. At the end of the two and a half hours, she said she was sorry they didn't get to sing the music, but it would just heighten their anticipation for the next week. Wrong.

Exercise 5: What is TMI for Your Chorus.

Only you can really know what your singers can handle in the way of information. Once you have done your homework, go back and filter it out to what you think is truly interesting that sets this piece apart from all of the others they are singing and what part of the information will truly make a difference in the way they perceive or perform that piece. Just tell them that much.

Exercise 6: Know Thyself

There are many tools that will help you know more about your personality type. Perhaps you have already done one of these. One of the most common is the Myers-Briggs Type Indicator. These indicators are priceless for you in your own understanding of the process. Myers-Briggs has an incredible tool titled *Introduction to Type in Organizations*. It is a must read for anyone working with people.

If you love performing but not the time-consuming preparation; if you love the product more than the process; the end more than the means; if you gather energy from being around people; you are most likely an extrovert (E). You won't ever become an introvert (I). This is a person who gathers energy from being quiet and alone (practice room), but you must master some of the skills of an introvert, i.e., the quiet preparation

required to do your job well. The opposite is also true. If you are an introvert who loves score study but not so much the stage, you must learn the skills of the extrovert, although you will never actually become one.

If you gather information through facts and what is real and practical, you are Sensing (S). If you would rather rely on what could be an inspiration, you are categorized as Intuitive (N). At the same time, if you organize and structure information in a logical objective way, you are a Thinker (T) rather than a Feeler (F), who organizes in a personal, values-oriented way.

Finally, if your preference is for a planned and organized life, you are a Judger (J) rather than a Perceiver (P), who has a preference for living a spontaneous and flexible life. We conductors have to learn all of the above skills in order to be a success. Most of the singers in your chorus (and you) are probably ENFP.

In *Introduction to Type in Organizations*, the authors describe people falling in this category as people who are "enthusiastic, insightful, innovative, versatile, and tireless in pursuit of new possibilities. They enjoy working on teams to bring about change related to making things better for people." Among the potential pitfalls, are such things as "may overlook relevant details and facts, may overextend and try to do too much, may procrastinate, may move on to new ideas or projects without completing those already started." Among the suggestions for development are, "pay attention to and focus on key details, set priorities, learn to say "no" and apply time management skills to meet goals.

🏃 *Exercise:* Find a personality tool and find out more about yourself. This will lead you to understanding your singers, as well as learning more about how to motivate them.

Aural Modeling

What is in your mind's ear? Do you have a favorite choral recording? Do you even listen to choral music? You don't have to answer that out loud. However, whatever you listen to consistently helps set your tonal preferences for your own chorus. You know it when you hear it, you just may not know how to get there.

Your chorus will only sing as beautifully as you can imagine them singing. And only as beautifully as you are able to convey that imagined tone to them via your choral technique. But first comes that aural ideal of yours. There are choral techniques you obviously admire and some you avoid (or should).

Consider the aural modeling your singers have had in their experience: Brittany Spears, Randy Travis, and Jessica Simpson. We may pine for the good old days when we had Frank Sinatra, Peggy Lee or Perry Como. But we also had Johnny Cash and Ethel Merman.

Regardless of your opinion of the new pop/classical crossovers, thank goodness the public gets to hear what we would call a more "legit" sound. Do you play your favorite choral groups for your singers? Can you describe for them why you like the sound (and how you hope to achieve it with them)?

If they have not heard anyone "better" than themselves, they are striving toward a goal housed only in your head.

Exercise 7: Top Five

Choose your top five recordings. It can be a single piece or an excerpt from a larger work. Burn a CD with portions of your top five in one place where you can listen to them in a row. What is it that draws you to each of them? Is there a common thread? Does that tell you something about what you are striving for in your own work with your own choruses? You might want to play this for your chorus.

Exercise 8: Bottom Five

Now, just for fun and just for yourself, compile a CD with your least favorite five choral moments. Don't put the names of the performing groups on it, just in case someone finds it.

CHAPTER 9

Rehearsal tips:
plan your rehearsal
as if your
life depends
on it
(the life of your
choir certainly does)

REHEARSAL TIPS

PLAN YOUR REHEARSAL AS IF YOUR LIFE DEPENDS ON IT

(The life of your choir certainly does)

Rehearsal is the most important three hours of my week! Period. It is a time when I have been given other people's time to do with as I wish. It is a serious responsibility. It is not my time to whine or complain. It is not my time to let whatever is happening in my own life affect my performance in rehearsal. The singers don't need to know if I am tired or sick or just sick and tired. It is not their problem. My job is to take them out of whatever they are currently experiencing in their own lives and use the music we are making together to lift us all to a higher place. That can't happen if I begin with any disclaimer on my part. This has nothing to do with being vulnerable with your singer family. Of course, you need to be vulnerable to a point and let them share in your life's ups and downs. But not at the beginning of rehearsal.

Rehearse in Concert Order

From the very beginning of a rehearsal period for a concert, you have some idea of what you think the order of the concert will be. It is that recipe you are cooking up from the Parable of the Flat Concert Cake (page 107). Begin with the concert order in your mind and in their music packet from the very get-go. They will then have their music in concert order in their notebooks and that alone makes rehearsal go more smoothly as they are not searching for the next piece. A few times in the rehearsal period, you can go in reverse order, just to make sure you learn that final song!

We learned from our college days that we were best when we sang our recital through many times, in order, before the actual date. This has to do with pacing of the voice. This is equally important in a choral program. The singers (and you) need to know what the demands of the program are going to be far in advance of the actual concert. You may think this sounds crazy, but it will help you in every possible way imaginable. You may find that two songs you put back to back really don't work. And you have plenty of time to change them.

A.D.D.

We live in a fast-paced world. Everything we do is fast-paced. We are accustomed to multi-tasking with information coming at us all at once from many directions. It is the way we are, period. You can't fight that. And it has resulted in a great deal of attention deficits all around the room. For this reason, and several others, my suggestion is to divide your rehearsal in five-minute increments on your rehearsal planning sheet. As you will see from the sample plan in the back, there may be a song you want to spend 15 minutes on. If so, you must consciously mark through three of your five-minute increments.

A conducting student came in recently and stated proudly that he had prepared so incredibly well for his community chorus rehearsal that he had managed to spend an entire hour and a half rehearsing one song! He works with a volunteer community chorus. I congratulated him and told him the proof of his expertise would be clearly demonstrated the next week when half of his singers stayed home! They knew he was green, though, and showed up the next week when he had actually done a rehearsal on the five-minute increment plan. He was much happier and I know his chorus was, too.

Do not make them sit through too much note chasing. Never have one section of the choir spend half an hour on one section of the music while the others simply sit. It can only serve to defeat them musically and kill the morale. Find a way to divide them into sections to pound out notes. If you have to chase notes for one section, allow the other singers to lightly hum their parts as the section in question sings theirs.

Halfway through rehearsal, go back and repeat or pick a new exercise for breathing,

relaxation or one that has to do with the repertoire you have chosen for the last part of rehearsal. For heaven's sake, if you do an exercise at the beginning that relates to a piece you have scheduled to rehearse an hour later, they won't remember it.

Start and Finish

Begin your rehearsal in the most positive way possible and most importantly, plan the end to do the same. Don't just run out of time while you are in the middle of note chasing with the basses.

Progress Report

Depending on how well your chorus sightreads, you may be able to sing through all of the pieces on the very first rehearsal and achieve as much as 60 percent of what you are hoping for when performance comes along, If you continue to work little bits of most or all of the pieces, then the next week you will be at 65 percent. The next week it will get a little better and by the time the performance takes place, you may be at 90 percent for the entire concert and even 95 percent on some pieces. Working on one piece for an entire rehearsal may mean you get to 90 percent on that song, that week. But you left all of the other pieces right where they were at 60 percent. By skipping a week and not singing them, they will probably slip to 55 percent at best. At this rate, your concert is going to be horribly out of balance. You will have a few pieces that are great and a few that are horrible, because you spent all of your time on only a few.

And don't forget that if you have one rehearsal a week, you can spend a great deal of time getting one piece to 95 percent, but your singers go about their lives and will come back the next week at 75 percent. You have wasted their lives.

All of the pieces you have selected (and that remain throughout the rehearsal period) are your children. They need equal treatment. Otherwise, why did you choose them? Surely not a filler. When you have worked the horses hard in the field (or the cows or pigs) and the day is over, you head them for the barn and LET THEM GO. The same is true of your singers. You work them hard. At the end of a long work session, head them for the barn and let them sing! Save the last minutes of your rehearsal to just let them sing. It's what they are there for!

Instant Clinic (with no fee for clinician)

Divide and conquer. Divide your chorus into halves, regardless of how small or large and have one half perform a piece for the other half. They will invariably be tougher on each other than you ever would be. When the

second group performs, the "judgers" are then compelled to perform and demonstrate all of the things they corrected in the first group.

Changing from Rehearsal to Performance Space

Singing is kinesthetic, or muscle memory. Your singers can only reproduce sounds when they "remember" the correct ones learned and sung in rehearsal. They must know that the sound they make in rehearsal is the one they are to make in performance. It is your job, not theirs, to make any adjustments for a new room, different circumstances in performance, etc., not theirs.

To Memorize or Not to Memorize, That Is the Question

You know, there is just not enough time to debate this here. And since this is not a debate, but one person's opinion, there you go.

The reasons to memorize are completely compelling. If we could simply listen to two choirs singing the same repertoire back to back, one with music, the other without, the answer would most likely be clear. Most of the reasons not to memorize are not so clear. Bottom line is, except for major works, not memorizing is only laziness on the part of someone. There is no debate about the communication level of using music or not using music. This includes communication between you and your singers, and between your singers and the audience that took the trouble to come hear them perform. Music folders set up a barrier between performer and audience. It tends to make the experience an objective one for the audience rather than a shared, subjective one.

Singers using music squelches your own possibilities of music-making in many regards. Just because you rehearsed and rehearsed a certain way doesn't mean you are going to feel like that is the best for the performance. Be flexible (not always our best attribute). Allowing your singers to use music as a crutch removes all possibility of spontaneity and making music in the moment. If you suddenly try to make a change because it feels right at the moment, some of your singers will not be looking up and there ensues a mighty train wreck. We've all heard them.

Memory Tips

1. Sing every song every week. This means you may work on the details of a bunch of different songs throughout rehearsal, but you may not leave out songs for over a week. If you have only one rehearsal a week, this is difficult, but can be done.

2. Give pop tests. Just when they least expect it, have your singers put their music down.

They will surprise themselves (and you) at how much they remember.

3. Memorize the end of the piece first. That way, the singers will know the end best, instead of least, and breathe a sigh of relief when they arrive.

4. Cheat sheets. Pass out sheets with all of the texts written as poetry (which, of course, it all is). This is a great way to wean your chorus. It is also a way to get them familiar with the text itself.

5. Hand out a memory schedule in advance. Let them know what is expected and when. You can't memorize an entire concert and expect that the first time they will sing it from memory is dress rehearsal. I suggest a schedule that includes one easy piece and one hard piece per week leading up to the entire concert memorized at least two weeks before the performance. *Brag:* my chorus memorizes a two-hour concert approximately every ten to twelve weeks and they are all volunteers.

6. If you are frightened about going cold turkey on the memorization, try it for half of a concert. Either let the chorus use music for the other half, or share the concert with another interesting ensemble.

7. Always begin by being firm and convincing the singers you are serious about no music. If you have the slightest lack of confidence, they will see it in your eyes and hear it in your voice and they know you will cave in at the end.

Exercise 1: Memory Tips

Take your next program. Make a list of attainable memorization dates. Plan your rehearsal well in advance so you can hit every song every week. Make cheat sheets of all of the texts.

Exercise 2: Five-course Meal

We are always in a hurry to get on with the rehearsal. If we think of the warm-up period as a hearty meal necessary to do the work that follows, we will not starve our singers. Look at it as a menu at an incredible restaurant where you were going to have a five-course meal. You wouldn't select five appetizers and nothing else. Choose one from each group representing the areas of concern:

1. Posture (Chapter 2)

2. Motor (Chapter 3)

3. Vibrator (Chapters 4 and 5)

4. Resonators (Chapter 6)

5. Singing (Chapter 7)

🏃 *Exercise:* Plan a five-course rehearsal warm up using the template in the back of the book.

Exercise 3: The Plan

You are only as good as your plan. Imagine building a house with no plan, or building a house with a bunch of helpers standing around wanting to help, but with no tools and the only plan is in your head. That's not going to be a pretty house.

🏃 *Exercise:* Make a plan for your next rehearsal, using the template in the back of the book.

Exercise 4: Vocal Landscape

A vocal landscape map is a great tool in your own preparation. Such a landscape tracks the contour of the piece, the loudest and softest measures, difficult sections, text setting, etc. Vowels or leaps or chords that may be challenging can be included. The landscape will assist you in the creation of vocalises for each of those places. You will be amazed! See the example on page 144 on Joseph Martin's "The Awakening."

🏃 *Exercise:* Select a piece of music you are currently working on and do a thorough landscape analysis. Once you have done one, you will get the hang of it and it will come naturally.

CHAPTER 10

Things they didn't teach you:
tlc

THINGS THEY DIDN'T TEACH YOU

TLC

I feel sure you already know from my bio that the early part of my career was spent conducting both college and church ensembles. The last 18 years have been spent with volunteer community choruses. This has colored my opinions and my work tremendously. You will notice it right away.

Take a Visit to the Cafeteria

Just as you have already done, I ask you to approach the remainder of the book as you would a trip to the cafeteria. Get your tray and head down the line. Take only the items you think you like and will use. Leave the others for someone else. You may not like brussels sprout, but someone will. Remember the nice cafeteria lady with the hairnet pulled halfway down her forehead is just offering you a wide array of options because she can. And it's always fun, at least in Texas, to hear "Gravy on that?"

Making the Leap and Taking the Plunge

For almost all of us, our choral training wheels were found in either school or church choir. And those training wheels have served us well. Church and school choirs still provide some

support, a safety net of sorts. When some of us got older, we found choral music outside the confines of school and church: community choruses, symphony choruses, etc. They are hugely different.

Certainly, in church and school choirs there is the "safety net" of a larger umbrella organization that takes care of a great deal of the administrative and financial issues involved in running a choir. This is brilliantly addressed by **Chorus America**. But church and school choirs also have motivational tools not found in "stand alone" choral organizations. Both are tied up in "G" words.

In school, the "G" word is a grade. A very useful tool to motivate. In church, the "G" word is guilt. Another useful motivational tool. I felt you twinge from across the country. But sometimes the truth hurts. Whether or not you use the above to motivate, they are there if you need them.

In a completely volunteer community chorus, there is no such tool to get the singers to return week after week and also pay dues to do it!

It is a question of motivation. It has been my experience, since I have done all three, that in school and church and for the audience of the community chorus, you are only as good as your last concert. But in motivating the volunteer chorus to continue to sing, you are only as good as your NEXT concert. The afterglow of a good concert dwindles quickly, actually as soon as you pass out the music for the next one. The singers' enthusiasm is only perpetrated by what is the next choral carrot you are dangling in front of them

I have seen more people crash and burn when making the leap to a volunteer chorus outside the above mentioned institutions and their safety nets. In addition to the laying out of plans and goals and concerts and excitement and tours, there are really several dynamics that must be present to help make that transition:

❖ A well-articulated mission/vision statement for the group.

❖ A feeling of belonging, and that giving so much time and money to a hobby is worthwhile.

❖ Interesting, innovative, fun, and challenging programming.

The Parable of the Flat Concert Cake

We all cook. Regardless of how little we cook, we all know how to pick up a recipe and make something, even if it is out of a box. We would never think of just going to the cabinet and start throwing things together that had

no rhyme or reason. What if you just threw in all dry ingredients? What if you only threw in old ingredients. In the same manner, what if it were all wet, mushy, soggy items? What if all of the ingredients were things you couldn't even pronounce?

Well, every time you put together a concert, you are creating a new recipe. Hopefully, a recipe for success. You put all of the ingredients (pieces) out on the cabinet (computer) in preparation. Then you carefully put them together, in the order prescribed. Let's say you are making a cake (concert) and you put it all together as you thought it was to be done, you allowe it time to cook (rehearsal period) and finally it is time to unveil the finished product.

You take it out of the oven with a crowd of people anxiously awaiting the delicious treat (of your concert). And the cake is as flat as a pancake. But, because the crowd is gathered and the cake is not exactly rancid or dangerous, you offer it to them anyway. They go home unsatisfied, and worse, they tell everyone they know not to come to your house (concert venue) to eat your cake (concert). It takes a long time to regain their trust—if you ever do. They don't remember all the great cakes (concerts) you made before that, but they sure remember the "pancake cake".

Regardless of the dish you are cooking, add TLC to every concert. Yes, we all know that those initials stand for "Tender, Loving Care." And that, of course, is important. But more importantly, they also stand for the triple threat of programming:

TEAR...LAUGH...CHILL BUMP.

Think about it. Think about your own experience at concerts that have really moved you and perhaps even changed your life. It is possible that the concert contained just two of the above, but more than likely, it had all three.

> *They may not remember what you sang, but they will never forget how they felt.*

Programming Your Concert

As far as programming for community choruses, we were ruined in our academic training years ago (sorry, fellow professors). The fact is that in university choral programs, there is no compelling reason to worry about flow or pacing or "moving" the audience along. These are not things that are top priority. Nice if it happens, but if not, the conductor will not be judged lacking. So, we fall back on the most logical plan: chronological. "Why? Because we like it."

Sorry, but that is taking the easy road. Bear with me.

Competing for $$ and Attendance

Gone are the calm, good old days when people had plenty of time and enough money to do most of the things they wanted to do. We now live in a fast-paced world where we budget our time and our money much more carefully. This certainly has an effect on what we do as presenters of choral concerts. When you have scheduled your choral concert, just look at the options people have on the same night as your concert: a Broadway musical, a football game, a great television series final episode, an opera, a play, and an orchestral concert. What will get people to come to your concert, other than the family members of the singers, who are sometimes split by multiple events involving multiple family members. If you have 50 in your choir, can you guarantee 50 in the audience? And why would someone pay to hear your chorus when they can hear great choral singing in local churches and schools?

Cookie Cutter Choral Concerts

One thing is for sure: they will not keep coming back to "Cookie Cutter Choral Concerts" where the only thing that changes is the actual music in the folders held by the singers. Gone are the days when people show up to hear choral music for choral music's sake. Gone are the days when a choral group can sing one concert after another in the same hall, on the same risers, in the same black formal attire, with the same black music folders and with the same expressions on their faces. You need to be creative. You can do this! You need to think about what would keep your own interest if you were the patron who paid $10 or even our top price of $53 per ticket (choral groups in other markets charge considerably more than this).

BREATHE! LET GO OF THOSE LITTLE DEMONS SAYING:
"We've never done it that way before!"

You know you can use the very same cookie dough recipe and make all kinds of different cookies with it by just adding one new ingredient!! Take that simple Toll House cookie recipe and add nuts one time. Another time, switch the chocolate chips for peanut butter chips. You know it works with M&M's. But the basic foundation is the same.

How does that relate to a concert? Start with simple things. Break up the choral concert with a small group or a soloist or an instrumentalist. Let the chorus members wear something different for the second half. Get rid of the risers if you are in a hall where you can do that. Otherwise, move around on them when possible. Use a surprise prop in one of

the numbers. We have begun to experiment with claps and snaps when appropriate. You can even go a little further than that without endangering the lives of anyone. Start the entire concert with an empty stage and a soloist, and add singers a group at a time until the entire chorus is in place. Allow the audience to participate. If you don't want to let them sing along at the holidays, have the singers sing "Jingle Bells" or "Silver Bells" and ask the audience to take out their car keys and "play" them whenever they hear the word "bell." They will never quit talking about it.

Engaging the Audience and Practicing with the Emotional Line

There is an emotional line that exists between singer and audience member. It is the place where the two meet and share the experience completely. Our hope is that the singer and the listener meet at a line that is midpoint between the two, where both parties are fully engaged. We want both of them to be emotionally involved in the performance. If the singer steps beyond that line in his/her own experience and becomes too emotional during the singing, the audience automatically pulls back, becomes less involved and more of a spectator than a participant. This happens, for example, if singers get so emotionally involved that they cry or overly express the music.

On the other hand, if your singers do not involve themselves in the expression of the text and the emotion of the music, the audience mirrors their lack of engagement and once again will immediately detach from the experience. They will sit back, unmoved, and become judgmental, to boot. The real magic is for the performer and audience to meet exactly halfway and share the experience equally. My personal belief is that your singers will never approach that line with the audience if they are holding folders (except for major works or extended foreign language pieces). I think the use of music tucks that emotional line, where the chorus might meet the listeners, neatly away in the side pocket of the folder, out of reach.

 Exercise: In order for the chorus to find the emotional line, I will ask them to overstep what they know is that line. If we are singing a song that is emotionally gripping, I will ask them to focus on someone they have lost, be it friend, relative or pet. I ask them to go ahead and fully experience all of the emotions that go with those thoughts. It doesn't result in very pretty singing, but certainly helps the singers attach an emotional response to the singing and identify the line beyond which they are not to go in performance.

The Talking Conductor

Most people in the audience want to hear the conductor talk at some point. If you don't say a word, or if no one says a word, there is a disconnect. The performers don't seem like real people. I have heard incredible choral concerts where no one said a single word. In ways, I felt I may as well have purchased the recording.

However, no one wants to hear the conductor talk between every single song or piece. I repeat, no one. Well, except maybe the conductor's mom. And the worst phrase a conductor can possibly utter is "This next song is about…" **Don't ever do it**.

There is nothing more amateurish (in the bad sense) or condescending, for that matter, than to remind the audience that after every single song another is about to happen! They know that. They have a program, for heaven's sake. The only possible response to that is "Duh!" You have spent hours being creative with the music on your program. Spend at least that much time being creative about what you, or someone else, is going to say. Planning is the key. Few are able to simply "wing it." And don't read it, either. You are going to memorize your music, so you or the narrator can memorize the spoken words as well. If you are uncomfortable speaking, then choose someone from your chorus to "narrate." Save the history and analysis for the program notes! This is not the time to read from Groves or

Grout. Lastly, try not to open a concert with talking or announcements or a welcome. The audience came to hear music. At least let them start by hearing music. Save the talking for after the first piece or just before intermission, if there is one.

The Do's and Don'ts:

Don't start late.

Don't begin the concert with someone talking.

Don't allow the audience to applaud after every number.

Don't speak after every number.

Don't bow after every number (you or the choir).

Don't wait for the applause to end before changing the formation, the setting, the instrumentalists, etc. MAKE ALL CHANGES DURING THE APPLAUSE.

Don't end the concert with talking.

Don't allow your singers to wave at the audience at the end of the concert. They will look like a gymnastics team leaving the gymnasium floor.

Don't allow your singers to applaud for each other. All performers are performers.

All of the above will absolutely KILL the flow and professionalism of your concert. The whole point is to take your audience on a musical journey through all of their emotions. This journey is one that is planned by you—carefully. If you allow the audience to applaud after every piece, you are restarting the journey, the emotion, the flow. It's like leaving on a nice family vacation and stopping at every rest stop, truck stop, and historical marker. YOU WILL NEVER GET WHERE YOU ARE HEADED, you'll be so exhausted from starts and stops!

Thematic Programming

Regardless of what type of choir you are working with, you need to at least consider thematic programming. This can be as creative as you wish it to be and can be centered around countless things. You can center programs around texts, lyricists, composers, periods, times of year, countries, genres of music, and on and on. This does not need to be something that you find abhorrent. It is a way to connect the dots for your audience and keep them coming back.

You are not going to engender a great deal of excitement or interest in inviting people to simply come to the "Spring Concert" or the "Summer Concert." These are those dishes you cooked up without much thought and just pulled ingredients from the cabinet at random, making a dish from totally unrelated items—a little milk, a little vinegar, a little sugar, a little liver. After all, these are the things that were already in the kitchen (i.e., music library) and I didn't have to go shopping for anything new (i.e., work very hard)

Baton

Can we talk? I know this is going to be controversial, but it remains a mystery to me. Most authorities agree that the intent of using a baton is for:

1. Clarity of beat pattern
2. Extension of the hand so that large forces are able to see the baton in their peripheral vision. This would include singers over their folders or instrumentalists over their stands (as if they were going to look up anyway).

There are outstanding and famous (not always one and the same) choral conductors who swear by the use of batons for choral singing. No one has ever been able to give me sufficient rationale for it, though. I have watched hundreds, if not thousands, of conductors. Very few have been successful in communicating artistry to their singers when using a baton with a small to medium choral ensemble.

When my goal is ultimate communication with my singers and sensitive delivery of every word of text, why would I trade in ten human fingers for five and a stick?

My personal rule is: Use a baton only when my chorus is over 250 singers or there are ten or more instrumentalists accompanying. Other than that, my hands, my face and my body are all I need. In my opinion, the baton will limit your expressiveness.

Suggestion: Use your baton in a themed floral centerpiece on the mantel, except for the two times a year you need it to conduct. It will remind visitors of what you do for a living and remind your family members who is conducting business in the household.

Size Matters

In the case of conducting a chorus, smaller is better. I learned from a band director that if the group is not watching or following, the answer is to make the beat pattern SMALLER, not LARGER. The less they watch, the bigger we ordinarily make our beat pattern, assuming that they just can't see us! It works, in fact. When you begin to make the pattern smaller, they will actually look up to see what you are up to! Try it. Before my chorus goes on tour or sings for conventions, I have someone videotape me from the back during an entire concert. The only time I really want anyone behind me to see my gestures is if I choose to let them. Other than that, I am conducting for the chorus, not for the audience! Just try it. You may be surprised how effective and efficient your conducting will be.

"Negate"

You don't have to beat every beat of every measure from the first note to the last. You only have to conduct when someone needs you! Imagine a couple of beats go by in the music where you are not needed. I know it hurts, but it happens. Deal with it. If you have a competent accompanist, it is insulting for you to turn to them with a huge preparatory beat and, facing them so the audience can see your every move, conduct them through the entire introduction. What are you thinking? That at some point your excellent, well-rehearsed accompanist's body is suddenly going to be occupied by a stranger who takes control and goes crazy when you are not looking? Give a tempo and let the accompanist do his/her job. Same thing at the end. You don't have to control everything (I can't believe I said that). Then, you need to look for times in the middle of the music where you are not needed, and relax. If you are unable to stop conducting completely at those times because of some long-held belief that the world will stop if you do, then NEGATE, meaning keep up the beat, but keep it as small as humanly possible.

The Choral Bow

I wonder where the tradition of not allowing your chorus to bow started. If I knew, I would give them a piece of my mind. Yes, you did a great and mighty task as the conductor and you deserve all of the accolades you can muster. But you don't deserve all the accolades by yourself. Your singers worked hard as well. Let them take a bow for heaven's sake. Why wouldn't you? There's that answer, "Because my high school choir director didn't do it…or college…or whatever." Not a good enough reason. But don't have them bow after every song; just as you are not going to let the audience applaud after every song; just as you are not going to talk between every song. It is certainly acceptable for you to take a bow when appropriate and allow the chorus to bow at the end of the half or the program. Just don't leave them out.

All musicals and plays and operas choreograph the final bows as seriously as any other portion of the program. Why don't we choral directors do the same. All others begin with the leads or principals (OK, that's us). Then they move to any groups or ensembles or lesser luminaries. Then there is ALWAYS a "Company Bow." What do we do? Take the bow as the only principal. Give a nod to the lesser luminaries such as accompanist or soloists, then for the "Company Bow," it's back to US!!! No wonder we have the reputation of egomaniacs.

Suggestion: Have the singers count as they bend forward from the waist. One, two, three, four and up, two, three, four. This will give them a very dignified, rather slow bow. They will also be together. They will ask if they can count out loud. The answer is "Yes." You will never ask them to do this bow in silence!

Assigned Seating in Rehearsal

This is something that works very well for school or professional choirs. Sometimes, those of us who work in community or church choirs think it will work there as well. It has been my experience that it does not. Part of the reason our singers volunteer their time to sing is for a social outlet. They may join with friends or because of friends, or to make new ones. While assigned seating may sound good to your ear, the singer may not really like the people with whom they sound good. It is important that they enjoy the one, two or three hours they are going to spend in your chorus. I recommend placing only those singers that might be potential tonal problems. Again, find the balance between the social and musical aspects of your chorus.

So, You Want to Sing and Conduct?

This is one of the biggest things they don't exactly tell you in school. It is something we notice, but it doesn't sink in until later. We study singing in college. We hone our skills and work hard to develop our singing voices. Then we begin to conduct or teach. And what happens? We begin to lose our voices. Hmmm....where was that on the warning label of career choices? The more we conduct, the worse it gets. Then we look around at other conductors. Well, most of them came from instrumental backgrounds.

Another lightbulb goes off. The instrumentalists could burn the midnight oil in school and still practice the next day for hours. If we singers, however, did that, we paid for it in our voice lessons or in choir. So what does this have to do with anything? Having begun my career as a solo singer and then moving gradually into conducting, my own singing began to suffer. For a couple of days after conducting a three- or four-hour rehearsal, I couldn't sing so well. It is the same for teachers. For those of you experiencing these frustrations, the key is recognizing it for what it is and working for balance. Life is about choices. If your first love is solo singing, there are sacrifices to be made. One of those may be limiting your conducting if your singing is compromised. Otherwise, you may just frustrate yourself in the pursuit of two careers that are not particularly compatible.

Straight tone is a vocal style, not a lifestyle.

Straight Tone Singing:
A Few Words from the Experts.

"A proper vibrato is a sign of a healthy, well-produced singing voice. No kind words are forthcoming with regard to its (straight tone) coloristic advantages: straight tone has imbedded itself all too comfortably in certain vocal styles to be in need of further encouragement."

Richard Miller

"A fluid and even vibrato is certainly an indication that things are going right."

Barbara M. Doscher

"A recognized weakness of progressive education was neglect of the gifted child. In vocal music, the gifted singer is the one with vibrato. Such singers, however, stood out in the mass mediocrity which was called the 'a cappella choir,' and either the singer learned to inhibit his vibrato (and, incidentally, his talent and his personality) or he was asked to leave."

William Vennard

"Without some kind of pulsatory movement, vocal tone is inefficiently produced and harmonically impoverished."

Cornelius Reid

"Voices lacking vibrato are usually described as breathy, dull, straight, spread, or yell-like. One explanation of the vibratoless tone is that the intrinsic laryngeal muscular tension causes the mechanism to be rigid or static, instead of the relaxed and flexible condition necessary for proper vibrato functioning.... excessive straight-tone singing can retard the vocal development of young singers."

Clifton Ware

No authority I have found disagrees with the fact that a free vocal instrument has natural vibrato. Then why do so many conductors insist on their singers ignoring this in order to achieve straight tone?

Many reasons are given. Some have to do with being stylistically correct. Some have to do with better tuning in a choral setting. Both of these are legitimate. But I believe much of it simply has to do with the aural modeling a conductor has had, as well as the simple fact of what he or she was taught. It could be that they heard a chorus sing with straight tone and liked it and now demand it from their chorus, without careful consideration of what it might be doing to the singers' voices in the long run.

I like some country music. I like some Broadway and some gospel. I like some opera, lots of oratorio and lieder, and I like some straight tone choral singing. I don't like just one of the above. And yet, there are choral conductors who are so adamant about straight tone singing as to ignore all other possibilities. It is not stylistically appropriate to sing straight tone on all repertoire, just as the opposite is true.

Let's go back to the pendulum and the balance factor for a moment. In all things, there must be balance. If you want an example of stunning "straight tone" singing that moves the heart and caresses the ear, listen to any recording out of Brigham Young University. My favorite is the collected works of Eric Whitacre. Stunning, healthy singing. This is as straight as a tone needs to be.

Solo Singing vs. Choral Singing

You can just imagine the fine lines I have walked in my career as both voice teacher and choral conductor. Straddling both camps has been a lifelong exercise in being politically sensitive.

"Does singing in a choir five hours a week hurt my private study and my desire to develop my solo singing career," they ask.

Well, that depends first of all on the methodology of the choral conductor. Certainly, if he or she subscribes to the use of the full voice in the choral setting, it is a different deal altogether.

There is quite a simple answer for vocal students who are seeking solo careers (although not an answer they automatically

like to hear). If they are singing five hours in a choir where the technique being required by the professor is not one that is consistent with their private study, the simple fact is they have to spend five hours a week in serious development of their solo voice to counteract those spent in choir to be at square one. Not only should they already be spending five hours in private practice, but it will help them once again keep balance.

As for the choral conductors who require their singers to sing straight tone for an hour and a half with piano as the loudest dynamic level, this is my comment. What you are doing is like going to the gym to work out and lifting weights for an hour and a half with only your pinky finger. Then you go away and come back in two days (choir rehearsal) and spend another hour and a half doing the pinky finger exercise again. Over and over. No person in their right mind would do this, because the big muscle groups are ignored and eventually will atrophy if not used. You must allow the full use of the vocal muscles for healthy singing and healthy choral technique.

Be Careful What You Say!

Those of us who have adults in community chorus settings are the recipients of many, many instructions singers have received through the ages.

Focus the tone! What do that mean? Is that a phonation issue (breathy) or a resonance issue (spread) or a color issue (white)?

Support with the diaphragm! That can't be done, regardless of how many times you have heard that said or said it yourself.

Place the tone in the mask. You may as well say place the tone on a platter and garnish with parsley.

Blend, you rascals! They have no idea what that means except to cut back and basically stop singing.

Don't just let that note sit there, make it go somewhere. And where did you want it to go, exactly? Next door, or down the street?

Sometime, record an entire rehearsal, especially when you are teaching technique. Go back and listen and see if you can fully explain every single thing you have said in instruction.

Expect the Extraordinary

When you approach the music you are making with your chorus, expect the extraordinary. If you don't, you will never achieve it. Assume you are going to make exquisite music and nothing less. This means taking risks. Your singers have taken a risk by putting their time and talent in your hands. They want you to do

something special, not ordinary, with it. This also means coloring outside the lines. Simply following instructions and doing exactly what the music dictates is not enough. Read the great reviews of incredible performances. Rarely do they say, "The conductor succeeded brilliantly in doing exactly what was on the printed page." More often, they say, "Maestro took the music and made it his/her own, bringing creativity and life to the score."

"Dynamics and tempo markings are just suggestions."

Love the Process, Not the Product

When you consider you spend perhaps 30 or even 60 or more hours in rehearsal for a two-hour performance, it had better be the rehearsals that you love more than the performance. If not, you are all going to be unhappy. If this is not something you have thought about, you can turn this around in your own experience. The best way to do that? Spend time planning your rehearsals and thinking about your own attitude and "performance" in rehearsal.

Music Is a Means, Not an End

If we are content to simply make music for ourselves, then why worry about inviting anyone? More than likely, if just perfecting a piece of music is enough, then the audience wouldn't really want to be there anyway. Music is the vehicle we have chosen for the journey, not the destination. The journey is the incredible part. Each week, individual singers attend your rehearsals. They bring with them a world of issues we don't have time to address individually. And they leave them at the door, smile at each other, put down their inhibitions and fears of embarrassment, and willingly become one with the others in the room. It is truly a remarkable thing. And it is life-changing for them. You are most likely a conductor today because you remember the time when you became "one" with the other singers, the conductor, and an audience somewhere along the way.

We have all heard "The way to a man's heart is through his stomach." Well, "The way to our audience's heart is through their ears." And it is their hearts we want to move. Sometimes we move them with the sheer beauty of the music. Sometimes we move them with the message. But the greatest fear of all is that they will remain unmoved.

It's a Choir! It's a Family! It's a Support Group!

Sounds like multiple personality disorder. But at any given moment, your chorus is all of the above and more! You choose the order and the appearance of the different personalities. Never forget it is a vehicle for socialization and social change.

Audience Development

Everyone thinks that audience development simply lies in the advertising. This is not the case.

Number One Key: Consistency of Product! Give five great concerts in a row, no one mentions it, not to your or their friends. Give ten great concerts in a row, they will be permanent fans and start talking. Give one bad concert, they'll stay away for the next five and tell all their friends.

Member Recruitment

Everyone thinks that member recruitment simply lies in the advertising. (Have you heard that before?) This is not the case.

Number One Key: Have a clearly defined mission/vision statement for the chorus. They need to know exactly what they are signing on to do and what are the parameters. We have our mission statement on a sign in the front of every rehearsal.

Member recruitment is internal and organic – not so much external. You can put signs all over town and ads in every paper about auditions. But it is what your singers are saying to their friends that really matters. If your singers are saying, "I can't wait until Tuesday night. It is the most fun, productive evening of my entire week," who wouldn't want to join them to see what it is about? If your singers are saying, "Oh, dear, tonight's rehearsal and I'd rather have a root canal," who is even going to give it a consideration?

Be Flexible

This is not one of the traits most often attributed to conductors. But it is certainly one that will make everyone's lives much happier. I know I told you earlier that every single piece in your repertoire is like a child. Then I told you to be willing to admit that one of the ingredients you chose to put in your concert recipe is not working and be willing to cut it from the program. And I mean be willing to cut it as late as dress rehearsal, even if it is in the printed program. You gain nothing by digging your heels in and subjecting your audience to a "half-baked cake." And your singers will not trust you the next time this happens! And what does this have to do, then, with each piece being a child? Can you just drop a child at the last minute? Well, having two of my own, I know the answer! At the last minute, if you have an

unruly child, you sometimes have to exhibit "tough love." That child (piece) has not behaved properly, for whatever reason. In that case, it would be wrong of you to allow that child (piece) to perform.

A Word on Boards

If you are conducting a community chorus, the board must not be made entirely of singers. They are not objective, in any sense of the word. Community leaders can be objective and love what you do. If the president of your board is your boss, and also a singer, and you don't give him/her a solo in the holiday concert, you probably won't be getting a smoked turkey for a holiday bonus this year. Think about it.

Organization

This may seem like overkill to you, but it works great for us. I think it will work no matter how large your chorus. Each of the four sections has two "leaders." Each section has a Musical Section Leader and an Administrative Section Leader. The Musical Section Leader is the one who is in charge of making sure the section has the music and the artistic information they need. They are the ones to receive the Musical Mishap forms as seen on page 148. The Administrative Section Leader takes the roll of each section and generally takes care of the nonmusical issues that arise. All of these are simply liaisons of the conductor, helping distribute the responsibility throughout the chorus. It also minimizes the number of questions and the number of announcements made during rehearsals.

Communication

As mentioned earlier, too much information can lead your chorus to overload regarding your research into the music you are asking them to sing. There can never be too much information, however, regarding communicating the countless details it takes to mount a choral program.

No doubt you already pass out information on a weekly basis to your members about rehearsals, performances, additional meetings, fund-raisers, etc.

Here are two other suggestions. Electronic phone trees are not expensive to purchase. You can have every single member on a phone system that will dial them all with updated messages. You can divide them into groups so you can phone one section, the officers, or any group you choose.

More important and current are e-mail groups. Every Tuesday night, we pass out a hard copy of important information in "Tim's Notes." The following day, we e-mail those

notes (sometimes updated from the night before) to every single member. This way, no one can ever say they didn't know about the schedule or changes or what to wear! If they don't know, they didn't read their notes, hard copy or e-mailed copy. For a time, we had a few members without e-mail, so we mailed notes to them. Now we are at 100 percent of the membership with e-mail capability.

Announcements in Rehearsal

There was a time when there would be a line of people who wanted to make announcements at rehearsal. Some had relevant things to say. Some just wanted to hear themselves talk, and most often about events that were three months away and had nothing to do with the chorus. This has been remedied by one person doing all announcements. If a person has not given their announcement to the appropriate person in time to be included in the printed notes, they give a written announcement to the officer in charge of announcements that particular night. The officer can then make a judgment if the announcement is urgent or timely. If not, it can go in the following week's printed notes! This has hugely curtailed lengthy and meaningless announcements.

Kudos

One of the things we do a terrible job of as conductors is passing on compliments to the chorus. Like taking all the bows, we hear the great things people say and often forget to pass them on. The e-notes take care of this. Each week, we add letters, comments, entries on our Web site guest book. This does not cost us a penny and it does wonders for the members to actually hear the compliments. Now, members will e-mail comments they hear so that we can include them in the notes. We can never boost our chorus morale enough. The words of others go a long, long way to motivate them to keep working harder.

Productivity Tool

Some years ago, our chorus got in the terrible habit of complaining behind the scenes. We were allowing this to continue and even encouraging it by not having a constructive outlet for complaints. Someone came up with the "Productivity Tool." It has literally changed our chorus. Of course, we all know that you should always "go to the person who can make a difference." You don't complain about air conditioning to the plumber or about your bad haircut to your dentist. But in choir, we complain all the time to each other. It is terribly destructive and counterproductive.

So, with the introduction of the Productivity Tool, we then gave each member a voice and a vehicle by which they can be heard. And each of them is answered. Sometimes the answer is "that is crazy." But, they feel their opinion was at least considered. We provide these at every rehearsal.

It replaces the "Suggestion Box" with a tool that is much more thorough and requires a solution. You can't just complain unless you have an idea how to do it better. And, more importantly, YOU CAN'T JUST SAY "A WHOLE BUNCH OF PEOPLE AGREE WITH ME." You have to write down their names. When people think they might get their name put on a productivity tool, they quickly stop agreeing and soon they stop listening. A copy is provided at the end of the book.

Musical Mishaps

Another incredible tool we use is the "Musical Mishap" form. It is a small form that we take to the local copy place and have them made into tear-off pads. These are in the back of the room and most guys have one in their notebook. With two hundred singers, we would never get through a single rehearsal if each person raised their hand just one time to ask for a note to be played or a rhythm to be clarified. We do have sectionals to learn notes. We don't learn notes in the full chorus rehearsals.

But occasionally, sectionals aren't enough. That is where the form comes in. If a person sitting in the middle of a section notices that they are not getting a passage, rather than raise his/her hand, they fill out the Musical Mishap form and turn it in to the musical section leader or to the conductor.

This allows me to go through the forms before the next rehearsal. I will either make a list of all of them and hit them all at the beginning of rehearsal, or I will write them in my rehearsal plan so that when we get to that piece, we hit that section first.

You cannot imagine how much time it saves and how great your chorus feels that you have addressed their "issues."

Attendance

This is always an issue in a volunteer chorus, especially one where each member pays dues in order to sing. It is difficult to say "If you don't come to every rehearsal, I'm going to make you stop paying dues." Something is lost in the translation. We have tried everything and finally have come up with the best system I have ever encountered.

The point, after all, is to make it possible for all the members to sing, but also not punish those who come to every rehearsal by

allowing someone to miss too many rehearsals and then perform poorly.

At the beginning of each concert period, the administrative section leaders, along with the conductor, determine the actual number of rehearsals for that particular concert. Let's say there are 15. At that point, they decide together what the threshold is for missing rehearsals. Let's say the decision is no more than three. There are people who may know up front they are traveling and will miss 4. But these are people who learn their music well.

Everyone is treated the same. When a person has missed their third rehearsal, they are then notified that they will be required to sing a Concert Preparedness Audition two weeks before the performance. At that point, the conductor and whatever committee of "judges" he/she chooses will listen to the group assembled to determine if they know the music well enough to perform. The audition is not difficult, but simply a hurdle that everyone knows they must clear if they are to perform.

With this system, the singers know exactly what is expected. They also know if something comes up and they miss more than 3, they are not automatically out of the performance if they do the required work. The singers who made all of the rehearsals know that you have required something extra of those who missed, so they feel good. The singers who miss more than three and know they don't know their music, usually bow out of that concert rather than embarrass themselves at an audition.

Musicality vs. Musicianship

This is a fascinating debate. Most agree that musicality is innate. Musicianship is learned. You have singers audition for your choruses that simply "get it" when it comes to communication and musicality. You have singers who take lessons for years, study ear-training, theory, and keyboard. In other words, arm themselves with all of the skills required to make music, yet are never musical. Sometimes, those born with the talent do not learn the skills. You get to deal with the gamut when you conduct a chorus. Balance is the key. Teaching both musicianship and instilling musicality are both worthy goals.

Partnerships...Go Outside the Box

One of the most rewarding experiences you and your chorus will have is when you think outside the box in programming and in collaborating.

Regardless of whether you are in a church, school or community chorus, there are opportunities galore just waiting for you. This is true whether it is with dancers, instrumentalists, actors,

children, ethnic music groups, and on and on. You, your singers and your audience will only be enriched by these kinds of events. Yes, it takes time and energy. But the payoff is worth it.

Interesting Factoids:

✤ According to a recent NEA Survey of Public Participation in the Arts, one in ten Americans sings in some kind of organized group. This means 20.3 million people are singing in groups! This is far more people than jog on a regular basis. Will we ever run out of singers? Not likely. We will run out of runners first.

✤ According to research done at the Center for Voice Disorder of Wake Forest University in Winston-Salem, NC, singing styles were graded according to laryngeal muscle tension. They were rated on a scale of 1 to 100, 100 being the most tense.

Here are the results:
96 – gospel singers
89 – hard rock singers
86 – country and western singers
65 – jazz singers
57 – opera singers
41 – choral singers!!!

If ever you wanted a case for why people should sing in a choir, here it is. How many times have you heard the studio voice teacher tell a student that singing in a choir will ruin his/her voice? Apparently not, according to the muscle tension scale! More on that topic a little later.

Why Do They Sing?

Humanist psychologist Abraham Maslow has formulated a theory of the needs hierarchy of humans. Most astounding is that 7 of the 8 basic needs of humans are covered by singing in a chorus!

1. Biological (food, drink, rest, oxygen, etc.)
2. Safety (create a place of safety and trust)
3. Attachment (with you, with each other, with listeners)
4. Esteem (pride in accomplishment)
5. Cognitive (making music improves I.Q.)
6. Aesthetic (art lifts everyone to a higher level)
7. Self-actualization (getting in touch with inner self)
8. Spiritual (sharing and giving of self)

This is a huge responsibility for you. There are few other experiences your singers can have that so thoroughly meet their many-faceted life needs. And if you have an occasional potluck, you can take care of number 1 and hit all 8!

> *There is no activity people can engage in that meets as many basic human needs as being in a choir.*

Exercise 1: Needs Assessment

Look carefully at the list. Which do you think your chorus provides its members? Which are your responsibility? Which can you improve upon to make your chorus a better functioning organization and the individual members feel more engaged?

Why Do They Sing for You?

Because they trust you. They have faith in you! Every time your chorus sings, it takes a risk. Singing is a very vulnerable thing to do. Polls have ranked things people fear most in their lives and have come up with death as number 1 and public speaking as number 2. I am sure singing in public, for many, is right there at the top of the list. Certainly it is much more of a risk than say, being on a bowling team. You can always blame poor performance on the shoes or the balls or the lanes or whatever!

There is a risk that they might not do their best or reach their potential. There is a risk of being embarrassed in public. There is always that risk that they might blurt out an unscheduled solo. They are trusting you. They trust you to teach them, direct them, protect them and lead them in doing something they could never do on their own. They are also trusting that you will respect them and the gift of their time and talent.

"To Risk"

To laugh is to risk appearing a fool.
To weep is to risk appearing sentimental.
To reach out for another is to risk involvement.
To place your dreams before the crowd is to risk ridicule.
To love is to risk not being loved in return.
To go forward in the face of overwhelming odds is to risk failure.

But risks must be taken because the greatest hazard in life is to risk nothing.
The person who risks nothing does nothing, has nothing, is nothing.
He may avoid suffering and sorrow, but he cannot learn, feel, change, grow, or love.
Chained by his certitudes, he is a slave.
He had forfeited his freedom.
Only a person who takes risks is truly free.

Anonymous

Yes, many will impose other roles on you: father, mother, brother, sister, pastor, etc. These are not in the job description nor your responsibility. Only you are in control of how many of these added duties you are willing to accept. Warning: if you accept them, no complaining later.

Conductor, mentor, teacher and guide are yours. When they put their unqualified trust in you, when they stand before you and share with you one of the most vulnerable experiences of their lives, it is both your love for the music you are making and respect for the gift of trust in you that will ultimately change both of your lives. And that of your listeners as well.

"Faith"

When you come to the edge of all the light you know, faith is knowing one of two things will happen: you will step on solid ground or you will be taught to fly.

Patrick Overton

Parenting Your Chorus

In the early stages of raising children, I was given some great advice that works with conducting a chorus as well. It is quite simple. When all is said and done, make sure you have given your children (chorus) equal amounts of discipline and love, never more of one than the other. When you sit back and think about it, there is a great amount of truth in that. You will never achieve greatness with your chorus unless you love them and love the music. On the other hand, you will also never achieve greatness with your chorus if you do not lead them with some discipline in your own approach to studying the music and conveying that to them.

Vocal health:
soup to nuts

VOCAL HEALTH

Soup to Nuts

Is it soup that is good for you and nuts that are bad, or the opposite?

Is milk bad and chocolate good? How about lemon or altoids?

Is artificial sweetener bad or should we really just eat meat and cheese?

In this day and age, we are all so incredibly conscious of what we are eating, it verges on the ridiculous. And how does all of this affect our bodies and our singing?

My teacher in Austria used to tell me that the oldest trick in the book, if you were an understudy, was to offer the person in the role a handful of nuts about a half hour before performance. In no time at all, they would be completely unable to sing and you would have your big chance at the stage! I never tried it, but it makes for a good premise for this little chapter on health.

I am not a medical doctor. I have been to many. I have several who are my friends and bail me (and my singers) out of precarious situations with our vocal health from time to time. This little chapter on health is not meant for you to take as the Bible of Remedies. It has some suggestions gleaned from many sources and

"checked out" recently with friends who are Pharmacist, Nurse and Physician's Assistant. Do not take my word for any of this. Use it as a reference only. Ask your own doctor for a specific diagnosis and prescription.

Most vocal problems result from
1. Short-term upper respiratory illness, such as cold, flu, sinus, allergies, etc.
2. Gastric issues
3. Vocal misuse and abuse.

Voice irritants:
POLLEN!
Inhaled Irritants: smoke, chemical fumes
Ingested Irritants: food, drink, drugs
Body Irritants: reflux gastritis, phlegm, adrenalin

When you are sick with an upper respiratory illness, treatment tips, for the most part, are only to keep you more comfortable while your body fights off colds, flu, sinus, etc. For example, rather than the shotgun approach of simply picking up something over the counter that will cover it all, be specific in your treatment:
Use a cough suppressant for coughing.
Use a decongestant to unclog head stuffiness.
Use an expectorant to release subglottal mucus.
Use herbal teas for the specific ailments they help.
Use antihistamines in worst case scenarios (see below).

Rest, stay warm, minimize stress, keep humidity at 40–50 percent, take vitamins, eat well, stop talking, HYDRATE.

If your doctor does not know you are a singer, tell him/her. They may be prescribing medication to dry you out not knowing you need something to counter that.

Nasal Decongestants may be the least damaging to your vocal folds to keep the secretions to a minimum.

Guaifenesin is your friend. This is an expectorant that will "help loosen phlegm and thin mucus secretions. It is found in most over the counter medications that say "Non-drying." It is also found in its purest form in "Robitussin" with no letters following such as DM or PE. Entex is a brand name drug that is sometimes given in tandem with drying medication. It contains guaifenesin.

Antihistamines: If you are suffering genuine allergies to substances (as opposed to sinus issues or a normal cold), you may indeed need an antihistamine. If so, use only a second generation antihistamine such as Tavist Allergy (Tavist Sinus is a decongestant). Do not use first generation such as Benedryl or Chlortrimeton. These are simply too drying. They not only dry up the problem area but every other single moist fleshy surface in your body, especially the vocal folds. The new nose sprays are great for allergies (Astelin, Rhinocort).

Recommendation to think about:

When you begin having abnormal drainage, feel a cold coming on, have pain or pressure in your head, begin a cough, etc. and it is absolutely necessary to stop or slow it, use one of the accepted medications listed above at night to keep the continual drainage off your vocal folds during sleep. As soon as you get up in the morning, begin the hydration process to replace the moisture literally sucked out of your body by the medication. If you can avoid taking the medication during the day, it would be best. Never take drying medication and then sing for an extended period. You will lose your voice. Nyquil at night is a wonderful thing.

Hydration: You cannot drink enough water. Hydration does not happen in the 15 minutes before a lesson or a performance. That is too late. You must drink consistently for several hours prior to singing to make any difference. A drink of water just prior to singing will not affect your vocal folds at all. It just helps with dry mouth. Only gargling will actually affect your vocal folds. Hold water in your mouth until it is body temperature, then gargle to remove thick mucus from the folds. The pharmacist also sells Alcohol, a nondrying, noninvasive gargle that can be used as well. (The admonition is to "Pee pale." If your urine is not as clear as water, you are not drinking enough water.)

Gastric Reflux: This is the latest diagnosis in probably 50 percent of all voice problems. It is literally the "backward or return flow" of stomach contents that back up into the esophagus or throat. LPRD (Laryngopharyngeal Reflux Disease) is reflux that makes it all the way into the back of the throat where it burns the sensitive tissues.

Treatment:
1. Get rid of stress in your life.
2. Pay close attention to reactions your body has to certain foods. This would include spicy, acidic, fatty (fast) foods. It also includes such beloved things as caffeine, alcohol, peppermint and chocolate.
3. Do not eat late at night.
4. Lose weight.
5. Elevate the head of your bed with boards or bricks. Simply using more pillows is not the best way to achieve this.
6. Stop smoking.

Medications such as proton pump inhibitors may be prescribed; such as Prilosec, Nexium, etc. Rolaids and Tums help, but they have calcium in them, which causes the stomach to produce more acid to counterbalance it. Gaviscon does not.

Personal Humidifier (not vaporizer):
At your local grocery store, you can purchase an individual humidifier. This is an incredible tool when humidifying your entire home is not an option. This is a simple device that provides steam just for you with a mask to cover your nose and mouth. A vaporizer with warm steam can cause problems because they grow mold and are seldom cleaned often enough.

Sinus/Nasal Flush: This is a last resort when things are really, really bad. For many, many years, a simple nasal snort of salt water has been a recommendation. The late Alan Lindquist did this every day of his life. This can also be done with a bulb purchased from the drug store. But for the real deal, here is your last resort. Purchase a disposable saline Fleet enema at the store. Drain and save three quarters of the liquid. Replace with distilled water. Leaning over the sink, or the bathtub, or in the shower leaning over, insert nozzle in one nostril, closing the other off…squeeze bottle as you inhale through nose. Hold the liquid inside for a moment. Alternate nostrils until bottle is empty. This will evacuate mucous as well as eliminate infection.

Chicken Soup, Hot Tea,
Honey, Lemon, Whisky.
These old wives' tales are pretty much just that. However, they are certainly not completely without merit.

Hot liquid passing through the throat causes the blood flow to that area to increase, which in turns speeds healing. Hot drinks are wonderfully soothing. Chicken soup has the added benefit of nutrients to help fight off the illness.

Honey and lemon are tasty and can soothe the back of the throat as well as increase saliva.

Whisky really doesn't do anything except make you not care so much that you are sick. If you are a bad patient, perhaps your caregivers are the ones who need the whisky.

None of these have a direct impact on the actual vocal folds or larynx because they travel down the esophagus, not past the folds to the trachea!

Hydrate: I know I already said this, but it needs saying again. All caffeine products are drying and will counteract your attempts to hydrate. Pee pale.

Emergency: If you are sick and simply must sing in a day or two, ask your doctor for:
Medrol dose pak: Cortisone
Z-pak: Antibiotic

The solution to pollution is dilution.

Attributed to R. Steele

Thanks to all of my friends who assist in keeping us all healthy here in Dallas, especially laryngologists Dr. Presley Mock and Dr. Wayne Kirkham. Thanks for reading this chapter and giving your blessing: Robert Steele, CRNA; Corianna Seelig, RN; and D. Trew Deckard, PA-C, MHS.

CHAPTER 12

The aging voice: it's gonna happen

THE AGING VOICE

It's gonna happen

Consider for a moment all of the activities you were potentially involved in during your youth. You sang in choir and perhaps played another team sport such as football or basketball. Maybe you played tennis, ran a marathon or even tried your hand at ballet or gymnastics. All of these seemed so simple then. In fact, a single day could involve choir rehearsal, marching band, swim practice, jogging, and fighting with siblings at night before bed.

And of all of these things, which of those are you still doing? Singing in a choir. Not too many 50 or 60 years olds still play football or dance. Sibling fights are now over the phone or e-mail. And yet, we have people singing in our choirs who are not just 60, but sometimes 70 or even 80.

So, a singer comes to you with faltering vocal ability or a wobble and proclaims his/her desire to regain the beauty of their voice when they were 25. Ask them how hard it would be to do gymnastics again at their age. They would certainly never regain their complete facility, but what would be the first steps of even beginning that process? With the basics, the beginning would be stretching to determine how much could be restored. Before even a somersault, there would be

fairly extensive work to get all of the muscles back and responding.

And what are the basics of singing? There is the toning of the entire instrument. What kind of shape is the person in? Are they willing to look at that first and begin to get their entire body into singing readiness? Next would be the breathing apparatus. The restoration of a well controlled breathing machine would take work since the aging person probably has not breathed for singing in a long time. All of this kind of work must take place before one ever gets to the actually vocal folds. The muscle antagonism required of the chest and of the abdominal muscles must be restored.

I find at this point in the description, most people have just glazed over and decided to go ahead and drive their choir director crazy with the wobble they have come to love. But perhaps you would like to know a little more.

Once the body is back in line, then we can look at the actual phonation. Some of the things that happen in the larynx are much like the things that happen in the rest of the body. There is no reason to believe that our knees and backs and arms would begin to be stiff and creaky but not your voice. Presbylaryngis refers to age related structural changes of the vocal folds. Some degree of vocal fold atrophy and decreased elasticity appears to be part of the normal aging process. In fact, some degree of vocal fold "bowing" is present in 72 percent of persons over 40 years of age. This bowing makes the voice breathy, rough, hoarse and softer. The tendency is for women's voices to lower and men's voices to rise in pitch and become reedy and thin as the years wear on. Lack of flexibility in several areas, including the breathing mechanism and the cartilage of the larynx is an issue.

Aging causes people to speak and sing much softer in most cases. These changes can cause older singers to overcompensate. According to Leslie Guinn of the University of Michigan, "the extra effort often results in a slow and wide vibrato when singing." He suggests that people suffering with such a vibrato can, indeed, reverse the effect with care. The suggested regimen is to hydrate first. Then 12 – 15 minutes of vocal exercises every day, paying close attention to proper breathing at all times. "Wide vibratos are often caused by singing too heavily." Guinn suggests singing on [a] with a slightly breathy straight tone at a very modest volume, increasing the difficulty of the triads and scales in a comfortable range.

This can certainly be done in a choral setting as well.

So, what to do? The real answer is to maintain good vocal health throughout your life by doing the things you already know to do. And if your aging singer hasn't done these things, it is never too late to start. Use proper vocal technique in singing and speaking.

Exercise – your body and your breathing
    mechanism
Do not smoke
Hydrate
Take care of acid reflux and upper respiratory
    problems
Be willing to change voice parts as your
    voice changes and ages.
Embrace a new sound, not the over-
    produced, over-vibratoed one.

APPENDIX

APPENDIX

SAMPLE PROGRAMS

Here are two very simple, yet varied programs that might fall into a Spring/ Summer setting. Regardless of repertoire selections, this will give you an idea of how to schedule memory, how to plan a rehearsal and even some thoughts on how to put a program together.

Many of us are asked from time to time to put together programs that are patriotic. Below is a sample that pays homage to both Canada and my state. Of course, you can mix and match arrangements you already have in your library or use these beautiful suggestions by Gaspard, Hayes, Albritton and new pieces by Gene Scheer and Greg Gilpin.

I have included several things in the second program that could be added to this shorter program. One that is very effective is the presentation of colors that can be provided by many local organizations. In order to add interest, suggested readings by a narrator or multiple narrators could include portions of The Declaration of Independence. Before "Arms Around the World," perhaps you have a community member who has recently received his citizenship and may want to say a few words. Caution: never let anyone "wing it." Period. Sit down with them and interview them about their thoughts. Then you write it out for them. Tell them they may then use their own words, but these are the thoughts you feel are important (taken from them) and the length of the narration.

MEMORIAL DAY PROGRAM

Star Spangled Banner   *Traditional*

O Canada   *Traditional*

America, the Beautiful   *arr. Marvin Gaspard*
(Shawnee A 2139)

Testament of Freedom   *Randall Thompson*
Movements 1 and 4
(E.C. Schirmer 2118)

The Great State of Texas   *arr. Mark Hayes*
(Manuscript)

American Anthem   *Gene Scheer*
(Gene Inc Publications 3692)

Arms Around the World   *William Gaither*
    Arr. Greg Gilpin
(Shawnee A 2157)

God Bless America   *Irving Berlin*
(Manuscript – TCC)   *arr. Anne Albritton*

SUMMER CLASSICS:
Around the World in 80 Minutes

This kind of program allows you opportunities for tremendous creativity in how you build it. The enormous depth of repertoire will also offer great fun. The Genee and Pfautsh pieces are hilarious, in case you don't know them. The foreign language pieces can be tailored to your own situation and the various national heritages represented in your own community. Invite some local groups to join you, whether they be musical groups, dancers, etc. Perhaps you can increase the number of nationalities with soloists from the area or even from your chorus. The narrations here are similar to the shorter program. We have had great success with a narrator simply reciting the excerpt from Ulysses during the introduction to "The Quest Unending."

Now for the even more adventuresome. Begin the evening with the flight attendant giving instructions over the sound system about "in flight" safety, including turning off cell phones and other electrical devices! At intermission, pass out small bags of peanuts or pretzels (having apologized for no more meal service!). Make the program look like a trip souvenir book or travel guide. And on and on it goes.

Star Spangled Banner   *Traditional*

O Canada   *Traditional*

Presentation of the Colors
Narration: Welcome to the world of music.

Buccinate   *Giovanni Gabrieli**
  (Lawson-Gould 51908)

Cantique de Jean Racine   *Gabriel Faure**
  (Hinshaw HMC-933)

Insalata Italiana   *Richard Genee*
  (Shott C 45-439)

Gracias a la Vida   *Violeta Parra*
                       Arr. Willi Zwozdesky
  (Chappell and Company, Incorporated)

Songs Mein Grossmama Sang   *Lloyd Pfautsch*
  Performed by a small group

Narration: Declaration of Independence by
multiple readers

Testament of Freedom   *Randall Thompson*
  Movements 1 and 4
  (E.C. Schirmer 2118)

Arms Around the World   *William Gaither*
                          Arr. Greg Gilpin
  (Shawnee A 2157)

Dona Nobis Pacem   *Giulio Caccini*
                        Arr. James A. Moore
  (Alliance Music Publications AMP 0512)

Narration: Ulysses

The Quest Unending   *Joseph M. Martin*
  (Shawnee Press A 2218)

*indicates use of music

Sample Memory Schedule:

If you have only one rehearsal a week, these are your goals. If you have more than one rehearsal a week, memory is due the week of the date below.

March 1: Rehearsals begin
April 1: America the Beautiful; Arms Around the World
April 8: American Anthem
April 15: God Bless America
April 22: Testament of Freedom, 1 and 4
April 29: The Great State of Texas
May 4: Sing entire concert from memory
May 11: Dona Nobis Pacem (June)
May 18: The Quest Unending (June)
May 20 – MEMORIAL DAY CONCERT
June 5: Sing through entire June concert in order with music
June 12: Insalata; Gracias a la Vida
June 19: Sing through entire concert using music only where indicated
June 27: Dress rehearsal
June 28: SUMMER CONCERT

Sample Rehearsal Plan: April 1

Upcoming Performances
(see programs attached)
Memorial Day – May 20
Summer Classics – June 28

Repertoire to Rehearse Tonight:

Memorial Day:
Star Spangled Banner
O Canada
America, the Beautiful – memorized tonight
Testament of Freedom, #1 and #4
The Great State of Texas
American Anthem – memorized next week
Arms Around the world – memorized for tonight
God Bless America

Classics
Buccinate
Insalata Italiana
Dona Nobis Pacem

Add Next Week:
Cantique de Jean Racine
The Quest Unending
Gracias a la Vida

Goals Tonight:
✧ Firm up memorization on America, Arms Around…
✧ Work on notes on God Bless America
✧ Introduce 3 new foreign language pieces for June
✧ Have fun.

April 1, cont'd.

Rehearse in the Order of the Particular Concerts

7:30 Warm-ups – chosen from five-course dinner

7:35 Cont'd.

7:40 America, the Beautiful: measure 72 to the end to check

  Pop Test: close your music, sing from memory

7:45 Movement #1 of Testament — Touch on any questionable sections; sing through

7:50 Movement #4 of Testament — Point out differences and similarities in 1 and 4, sing 4

7:55 The Great State of Texas — If you didn't stand for the national anthem, make sure to stand for this one.

8:00 American Anthem — Some note chasing on this one

8:10 Arms Around the World

8:15 God Bless America — Difficult arrangement…requires some work

8:20 Continue God Bless America

8:25 Announcements — We have now sung through everything for Memorial in order! Memory schedule below. After break, we will begin to add the "Summer Classics"

8:30 Walk around, visit with each other, take care of business

8:40 Play a recording of Buccinate so they have a context

8:45 Play it again and ask singers to sing along on vowels

8:50 Read text to Cantique de Jean Racine in English. Read or have someone read it in French.

8:55 Sing through it on a vowel of your choice

9:10 Sing through Dona Nobis Pacem – beautiful and relaxing

9:05 Fun intro to Insalata!

9:10 Continue Insalata…announce solo auditions in a couple of weeks

  MEMORY WORK: stand and sing (head the horses for the barn)

9:15 America, the Beautiful

9:20 Arms Around the World

9:25 Good night — A few minutes early makes them think you are the best, most organized conductor in the world.

Rehearsal Plan Template:

Date _____

Upcoming Appearances: Dates _____

_____

Repertoire to Rehearse tonight:

Concert: _____

Repertoire: _____

_____

_____

_____

_____

_____

Concert: _____

Repertoire: _____

_____

_____

_____

_____

_____

Goals tonight: _____

_____

_____

_____

_____

_____

_____

_____

_____

_____

_____

Have fun.

Rehearsal Cont'd.
(Rehearse in the order of the particular concerts)

7:30 Warm-ups – chosen from 5 categories

7:35 Cont'd.

7:40 _____

7:45 _____

7:50 _____

7:55 _____

8:00 _____

8:05 _____

8:10 _____

8:15 _____

8:20 _____

8:25 _____

8:30 Announcements

8:35 Mini-break

8:40 Warm down exercise

8:45 _____

8:50 _____

8:55 _____

9:00 _____

9:05 _____

MEMORY WORK: Stand and sing

9:10/ 9:15/ 9:20/ 9:25

Good night – a few minutes early makes them think you are the best, most organized conductor in the world.

FIVE-COURSE MEAL OF WARM-UPS

Select One per Group

Posture (Chapter 2):

_____

(shoulder rubs, shaking out, jogging in place)

Motor (Chapter 3)

_____

(still no vocal fold involvement)

Vibrator (Chapter 4, #5)

_____

(attack, range extension, freedom)

Resonators (Chapter 6)

_____

(work on vowels, tone color, articulation)

Putting it together (Chapter 7)

_____

(choral blend)

In your plan, create some warm-ups from specific pieces you will be singing during the evening. Certainly you can (and should) choose more than one from some groups, just don't leave any out completely, or you'll go away hungry.

Also select a couple for after break or later in the rehearsal.

MY "LAST MEAL" OF WARM-UPS

So, after a book of more than 120 warm-up possibilities, the readers who helped me asked what my favorites were. They wanted to know the ones I couldn't live without if stranded on a desert island and asked to lead a choir. Here they are:

Posture (Chapter 2):

Massage (2.3) and Kindergarten Fix (2.11)

Motor (Chapter 3)

Sternum Power (3.1) and Farinelli (3.2)

Vibrator (Chapter 4, #5)

Messa di voce magic (5.3) and Boo (5.10)

Resonators (Chapter 6)

Baby Bird or Swan? (6.5) and This Is a "Fah fah fahn" Day Today (6.15)

Choral Singing (Chapter 7)

Matching Vowels (7.2) and Tractor Pull (7.13)

Sample Landscape of "The Awakening"

Look at the dynamic landscape of the piece. This will help you and your singers know how to pace themselves. Point out other Opportunities for Growth.

1. Set the dynamic range of the chorus so they know exactly where a quadruple "p" is in their voices and where the fortissimo is.

    Pianissimo: Measure 39 and 73

    Fortissimo: Measure 50, 82, and finally 123

    At 123 make sure you save a little for a final crescendo.

2. Vowel challenge: The (i) in *Dream is everywhere!* Beginning at ms. 10

    Figure it out at the beginning and you won't have to fight it the rest of the way through.

3. Keeping the line going when the phrases are divided as in Measures 34 – 39.

4. Tuning challenge: Measure 43

    This is a challenge to hear the entrance and tune the chords

5. What to do with the bad vowel at Measure 53.

6. Textural challenge: Diction in measure 60

    1. Whispering in Measure 70
    2. Yield! Each entering part must project. Those already singing must be quiet!

        There is also a challenge of enough (k) on *Awake*.

        Beginning at Measure 76
    3. Legato and Dynamic Challenge: The last few pages are a challenge in several ways.

        Measure 89.

The text must be perfectly understandable, the melody must be completely legato and you must help your singers avoid the temptation of giving too much too soon. Use the Tractor Pull here. Set dynamic levels for the last few pages, pulling back over and over in order for the climax to be powerful at the end.

Landscape of "The Awakening"

Dynamics ⬤   Yield ▼   Challenges ⌐■

PRODUCTIVITY TOOL: A LIFESAVER

In order to make productive and constructive suggestions,
I would like to make the following observation regarding:

_____ Officers   _____ Board of Directors

_____ Artistic Staff   _____ Administrative Staff

_____ Associates   _____ Others (Please Specify)

My view of the problem:

_____

_____

_____

_____

_____

A solution I would like to offer:

_____

_____

_____

_____

_____

Others who support my suggestion (NOT REQUIRED):

_____

_____

_____

Signed: _____

If you would rather write something on your own instead of using this form, feel free to do so.
Please remember to include your suggested solution to the problem.

Please mail or hand deliver to the president or whoever you feel would be appropriate.

PRODUCTIVITY TOOL (Cont'd.)

Your input as to the operations of the chorus is WELCOMED, ENCOURAGED, NEEDED, VALUED AND APPRECIATED! This form has been devised to facilitate the flow of suggestions and get them to the appropriate persons with as little delay as possible. You need to fill out only one form. Copies will be distributed to the appropriate persons. Leave your completed and signed form in the appropriate mailbox in the office. Please list the names of people who support your suggestions.

Leadership Team:
The Officer team welcomes your input as to the running of the chorus. The leadership team meets regularly in addition to Board of Directors meetings, at which time they will gladly consider any suggestions you might have. The President of the chorus sets these meeting times and will gladly make your concerns an agenda item.

Board of Directors:
The Board of Directors is responsible for the general direction, policy setting and fund-raising for the chorus. The Board welcomes your input and eagerly invites you to its monthly meetings which are held on the 4th Thursday of every month. You always have the opportunity to express your concerns. Please let us know in advance if you intend to address an area not on the agenda. When you attend a board meeting with the intention of addressing a problem you've identified, please plan to offer a suggested solution to the problem.

Artistic Staff:
The artistic staff welcomes your input into the musical product of the chorus. The Staff is continually seeking ways to improve the musical product to make it more rewarding for both the singers and the audience as well as how to run the artistic side more smoothly.

Administrative Staff:
The Administrative Staff is constantly seeking ways to make the office and support of the chorus run more efficiently. Your suggestions are invited.

MUSICAL MISHAPS

Please circle the appropriate section:

S	A	T	B
(T1)	(T2)	(Bar.)	(Bass)

Title of song _____

Measures of concern _____

What is the problem? _____

_____

_____

_____

_____

_____

Please return to any of the following:
Conductor, Assistant Conductor, Accompanist, Musical Section Leader

Or

e-mail to the conductor.

Thank you very much for your input!

The Turtle Creek Chorale Mission

Regardless of what kind of chorus you lead, it needs a mission statement. Extremely important in any organization are short, medium and long-term goals. The short and medium are most often tactical; the long-term goals are tied into the mission of the group. Whether school, church or community chorus, any group needs to have the broad view of what they are about and where they are going. Often, a good leader simply listens sensitively to where the group wants to go and gets in front. Other times, the leader must exert his or her own vision and lead the group places the group never knew they could or would go. All of this is guided by some kind of mission statement, written or implied. We have certainly found that the more defined the mission statement, the happier the choir. I am sharing the TCC mission statement and core values as only one example. There are many, many others. Putting the mission statement out there all of the time focuses everyone on the task at hand and on the bigger picture.

A Mission of Excellence, Community and Diversity

The mission of the Turtle Creek Chorale is to entertain, educate, unite and uplift our audiences and members through music that is distinguished for its innovation, diversity and artistic excellence.

❖ ENTERTAIN - Presenting quality male choral music and other musical activities that make a distinctive and significant contribution to the musical landscape.

❖ EDUCATE - Celebrating a positive image of the gay community and partnering with artists and organizations that share our values and mission.

❖ UNITE - Attracting a diverse audience and membership and building bridges to a greater awareness of our shared humanity.

❖ UPLIFT - Touching hearts and changing lives in a nurturing and affirming environment through the universal and unifying power of music.

About the Author

Dr. Seelig began as Artistic Director of the Turtle Creek Chorale in July 1987. In addition to conducting four groups under the TCC umbrella, Dr. Seelig is on the music faculty at the Meadows School for the Arts at Southern Methodist University where he teaches voice and vocal pedagogy.

He holds four degrees, including Doctor of Musical Arts from the University of North Texas and the Diploma in Lieder and Oratorio from the Mozarteum in Salzburg, Austria. He has sung and conducted all over the world—from Europe to the Far East. He made his European operatic debut as a resident baritone at the Staatsoper in St. Gallen, Switzerland. Dr. Seelig made his solo Carnegie Hall debut in 1991 and sang the Mahler SONGS OF A WAYFARER accompanied by the Dallas Symphony Orchestra and Rudolph Nuryev. The Fort Worth Star Telegram says, "known as a fine singer, Seelig also cuts a thick slice of ham."

Under Dr. Seelig's leadership, the TCC has blossomed. When he began, the chorus had 40 singers, two part-time employees and a budget of $70,000. Today, the chorus has 215 singers, eight full-time and ten part-time employees and an annual budget of $1.7 million. The chorus was the subject of an EMMY Award winning PBS documentary, has been on the Billboard "Top Ten Classical Music" chart and holds the 2004 Guinness Book of World Record for the longest choral concert in history, having sung for over 20 hours to celebrate their twentieth anniversary.

The Turtle Creek Chorale has toured Europe, performed twice at Carnegie Hall, for eight ACDA conventions state (2) regional (3) and national (3) and the Southeast regional MENC convention. The group has 33 CD recordings, including two solo recordings by Dr. Seelig, *Everything Possible* and *Two Worlds*. Dr. Seelig continues a busy guest conducting and speaking schedule, with workshop appearances for a wide variety of groups across the country.

Dr. Seelig has been honored on many occasions. A few of these honors include University of North Texas Distinguished Alumnus, The Dallas Historical Society designation of "history maker of today," and the Dallas Theater Center's "pillar of the Dallas artistic community." In 1996, Dr. Seelig carried the Olympic torch as it traveled through Dallas, having been chosen as a community "hero." He has not run since.

He is the proud father of two incredible children.

After Dinner Sweets

After an incredible meal, it is time to just relax for a moment and savor the experience. Maybe a small truffle, or an after dinner drink and reflection. The meal (concert) was a great experience. Parts of it may have been better than others, but overall it was one of the finest. And what do I have to take away from it other than memories and calories? That is the big question.

Earlier in the book I wrote about music being a means, not an end, and that choral music can be used to change the world in which you live. That sounds pretty high and mighty, but it is the tenet by which I live and why I go to work every single day just to make choral music. It is why I have chosen it as my life's work.

I gave that very lecture, "Changing the World through Your Music," recently. Some weeks later, a conductor from the Midwest phoned to say her daughter had been in that class, relayed it to her. Also a conductor, and had she asked me what I meant and how to start that kind of mental process with her own choirs. I was a little shocked. After all, it was just a lecture, not a "how to." But it made me ponder how one moves toward such a goal. Here is some of what I discovered about it.

The beginning is that very desire to change the way you look at your conducting, your chorus, and what you are doing with the combined time and talent of your forces. A paradigm shift in thought occurs: we can affect change through our music. Obviously, church musicians are way ahead of us on this front. The rest of us are not just way behind, we aren't even in the ballpark. And it begins with you, not a committee or a board or officers.

The next step is for YOU to decide how you want to change your singers and your audience and what are the things you want them to experience through choral music. Again, no one but you can make these decisions, because the singers are following your lead, in every way. You are the one they look to for guidance and for vision. And it is you who will be selling this along the way. Yes, it is risky and courageous, but well worth it in the end.

There needs to be a practical word at this point. It will change you and your singers. That is the main goal. But the other ancillary things that accompany such a shift are things such as total singer engagement in the process, increased audience participation and interest, broadened funding sources, long-range altruistic goals to keep the entire organization focused and moving forward. At first look, you may think you can't "give away" your music because you need the income it produces. Let me just say that using your chorus in the way I am suggesting opens the doors to all kinds of funding.

Changing the World

So, how to start? Put it out there. Say it. Tell a few close friends. "I want to make a bigger difference in my world through the music I make." You'll be surprised what that alone will do. But, of course that is not all it takes.

Take a little time for yourself. Go some place where you can think. What are the messages YOU would like to impart through your music. When you are no longer here, what do you want them to say about you? He/she conducted the most perfect choral concert or he/she changed the community through music.

They May Not Remember What You Sang, But They'll Never Forget How They Felt.

That statement may hurt a bit, but it is the truth. So, you are in a quiet place. What are the things that you believe in that you would like to share with your chorus and audience? When you begin this list, they emphasize things that are important to you:

Peace; Family; Health; Children; Diversity; etc. Yes, it sounds like a Miss America platform, but it is much more than that.

Next, look around your community and open your ears and eyes. And you will also open the eyes of your singers to opportunities. Once you do this, and you may already do it, you will see that there are ongoing opportunities to use your music in such a way. You are no doubt already being asked to perform for various events around your city. These will always keep coming; it is what we do. Be aware of what is happening in your community. Be ready to change and shift focus with the current events as they unfold. It starts with the small things, but will soon explode for you.

In the broader picture, it is up to you to provide long-range plans and goals in this area. You don't have to state them specifically, but in general. In the big five-year picture, perhaps you could lay out one concept per year that you would like to emphasize more than others. Once you do this, I promise the opportunities will fall in your lap.

I have tried to keep my own chorus out of the book for obvious reasons, but as I lay this out for you, I can't do it without some specifics. Forgive me. Following the above list, it could look like this:

Year 1: Peace. This could include a concert on the theme of peace in our world and in our lives and community. There is so much incredible repertoire written that fits into this. Once you have suggested that to the chorus, they will take the lead. One concert is specifically geared toward the theme, but the entire year can take on that thrust. At the concert, a portion of each ticket, or free-will offering, will go to the Red Cross or other nonprofit organization. We raised over $15,000 in one night for the Red Cross.

Year 2: Family. This could last several years, but we'll do it for just one. Again, the repertoire is certainly there. One of the concerts includes the family members of your singers. Yes, they all come onstage to sing the finale. Throughout the year, different emphasis is placed on different family members, groupings and families of choice. During the year, a small group from the bigger chorus makes an effort to perform at places around the city, whether that is a shelter for broken families or a family spaghetti dinner. Maybe the group goes out to serenade Habitat for Humanity as they build a house!

Year 3: Health. Choose a health issue that is affecting your chorus members or one of their family. Take a year to work on it, to raise awareness, to raise funds. We have done this on several occasions and to HUGE success and life-changing results. We commissioned large works on both AIDS and breast cancer. *When We No Longer Touch* became the PBS documentary *After Goodbye: An AIDS Story* and we commissioned *Sing for the Cure* for the Susan G. Komen Breast Cancer Foundation. Dr. Maya Angelou narrated the CD. I could write a book on each of these experiences. It will change your life to do something like this.

Year 4: Children. You can just go to town on this one now that your thought processes have been let loose. Our big children's year was the commissioning of *Song of Wisdom from Old Turtle* on the best-selling book *Old Turtle*. It benefits St. Jude's Children's Hospital and has Marlo Thomas narrating the CD. At the concert we gave, admission was free if you brought a child. And each child was given a copy of the book. There were over 1,000 people in attendance. As we sang, the children, with the help of their parents, turned each page as we got to it. Those sitting above in the balconies said it looks like the flapping of angels' wings as they all turned the pages together. Year after next, we will make the Make a Wish Foundation our focus.

Year 5: Diversity. This is also ongoing. We have partnered three times in the last 18 years with the Male Chorus from the First Baptist Church of Hamilton Park, a suburb of Dallas. Their chorus has 100 African American men and this has been one of the richest experiences of our lives.

We now give around 50 benefit performances a year with various small groups within the chorus. The increased awareness in the city brings people to the full chorus concerts. The musical philanthropy we do brings in funds from many sources that we could not normally tap. We are able to staff the small groups with the money we raise. It is a wonderful cycle. But the truth is still there: if you don't give, you don't get.

So, I didn't think it was fair to give an instruction that I was not able to give you concrete plans for. Maybe this will get you started!

And, now, about you personally. I had a conducting student who just didn't "get it." What do I mean by that? Well, the mechanics were there, but there was no music. There was no soul. We worked on phrasing. We worked on expressing the text. We worked on dynamics. On and on it went. Finally, I stopped and said, "May I ask you a personal question?" Of course, he had no choice but to say "yes." My question stopped him in his tracks. "When was the last time you cried?" He thought and thought and couldn't remember. That told me everything I needed to know about his music-making. It wasn't just the crying. It was the void of all emotional attachment. To anything.

My questions to you are:
When was the last time you cried?

When was the last time you cried at the sheer beauty of music?

When was the last time you cried at the music you were making with your chorus?

When was the last time you experienced a laugh, a tear and a chill bump in one concert?

If you haven't experienced that in a long time, you are probably just going through the motions and you can't create such an experience for your singers or audience.

Every single thing that I do with my chorus has a purpose. Every piece of music we sing has a part in the bigger plan. Obviously not all music has a life-changing message. That is not the point. But I do believe that all of the music is there to help us hone our skills. The better we are at our craft, the more people will want to listen. And when they listen, we have the opportunity to change them. If not their lives, we can change that moment for them. It all fits into the big scheme.

We must believe. We must be vulnerable. We must be proactive and lead our singers and our audience to a place far beyond where they ever thought they might be taken by musical experience.

When all of this comes together, it is **The Perfect Blend** of what we do.

Turtle Creek Chorale
Sammons Center for the Arts   P.O. Box 190137
Dallas, Texas 75219-0137
214.526.3214   fax: 214.528.0673
Dr. Timothy Seelig, Artistic Director
www.turtlecreek.org

Imagine a world filled with music where people focused on harmony rather than their differences.

TURTLE CREEK CHORALE

The Power of Harmony

INDEX OF WARM-UPS